IMPACT Intervention Year 2

Stephen Monaghan and Melissa Blackwood

Published by Keen Kite Books
An imprint of HarperCollins*Publishers* Ltd
The News Building
1 London Bridge Street
London
SE1 9GF

Text and design © 2017 Keen Kite Books, an imprint of HarperCollins*Publishers* Ltd

10 9 8 7 6 5 4 3 2

ISBN 978-0-00-823844-5

The author asserts their moral right to be identified as the author of this work.

British Library Cataloguing in Publication Data

A catalogue record for this publication is available from the British Library.

Authors: Stephen Monaghan and Melissa Blackwood
Contributor: Charlotte Monaghan
Commissioning Editors: Shelley Teasdale and Michelle l'Anson
Project Manager: Fiona Watson
Editor: Jill Laidlaw
Internal design and illustrations: QBS Learning
Production: Lyndsey Rogers
Printed and bound by CPI Group (UK) Ltd, Croydon, CR0 4YY

Introduction

Impact Intervention is a new series of resources created by teachers and aimed at teaching assistants, classroom assistants, NQTs and time-strapped teachers.

The books include tried and tested ready-to-go activities that are intended for use with small groups of pupils to help scaffold learning.

The resources can be used to deliver pre-teach sessions, booster interventions or breakout sessions after lessons to pick up pupils who are struggling to achieve a learning outcome.

Impact Intervention can be dipped into as needed and used with minimal preparation.

The books contain:
- standalone sessions with activities that focus on an achievable part of a learning objective
- content that has been broken down into small steps so that it is easy to follow and deliver
- activities that can be easily implemented in a 15–20-minute session without the need to read through lots of information in advance
- probing questions, prompts and key checks to help assess pupils' knowledge and understanding
- support and extension ideas.

Each title in the series contains content that is robust, age-appropriate and adheres to the standard of the KS1 / KS2 English and maths programmes of study.

Contents

IMPACT
Intervention
Maths Activities

Messy numbers

Strand: Number – number and place value

Learning objective: To order numbers to 100.

You will need: number line (one per pupil), 100 square (one per pupil), number cards (1–100 or a selection of your choice)

1. **Say:** *Mr Messy has messed up all his numbers and needs help to put them in order.*

2. Draw a number line from 0–100 (marking the number lines in tens).

3. Show the pupils several numbers on the whiteboard (or use number cards if you have them), for example 24, 31, 97, 16 and 46.

4. **Ask:** *How can we arrange these numbers?*

5. Take pupils' responses. (They might say from biggest to smallest or they might concentrate on the tens or ones.)

6. Tell the pupils that they will put the numbers in order from smallest to biggest.

7. Explain that they will need to look at the tens number first to compare sizes. Then, if two numbers have the same tens, they need to look at the ones to see which is the largest.

8. As a group, rearrange the numbers on the number line in ascending order.

9. **Ask:** *Can you show me these numbers on your 100 square by using counters to cover the numbers?*

10. Repeat this exercise with more numbers.

Key checks: Are the pupils able to tell you how many tens and ones are in a number? Are the pupils using the correct vocabulary: order, more than, less than, biggest, smallest, greater than, lesser?

Extension: Repeat this activity with numbers to 200. Repeat with decimal numbers.

Support: Focus on numbers 0–20. Pupils to find them on a number line and 100 square. Then move to just a 100 square – emphasising finding the tens number first and then the ones number.

Number numerals

Strand: Number – number and place value

Learning objective: To read and write numbers to 100 in numerals and in words.

You will need: whiteboards, whiteboard pens, board rubbers, 0–9 number cards

1. Write 'Fourteen' on the whiteboard.

2. **Ask:** *Can anyone tell me what number I have written on the board?*

3. **Ask:** *Can you write the number on your whiteboard in numerals?*

4. The pupils should write down '14' on their whiteboards.

5. Write twenty, thirty, forty, fifty, sixty, seventy, eighty and ninety on the whiteboard and ask the pupils to write the numbers in numerals.

6. Write twenty-six, thirty-nine, twelve and fifty-six on the whiteboard.

7. **Ask:** *Can you write these numbers down in numerals?*

8. Allow the pupils time to write down 26, 39, 12 and 56.

9. Write 45, 87, 91 and 16 on the whiteboard.

10. Ask the pupils to write these numbers in words.

11. Repeat this process to consolidate learning.

Key checks: Can the pupils spell the written number (phonetically plausible attempts are fine)? Are the pupils using the correct vocabulary: digit, number, numeral, more, less?

Extension: Provide each pupil with four number cards (they may write them on their whiteboards to remember them) and ask them to create as many different two-digit numbers as possible.

Support: Pupils focus on the tens column, ordering and the language associated with each number. e.g. 21: twenty-one, 31: thirty-one. Ask pupils what has changed (just the tens digit).

Excellent estimators

Strand: Number – number and place value

Learning objective: To identify, represent and estimate numbers on a number line.

You will need: whiteboards, whiteboard pens, board rubbers, paper, pencils/pens

1. Draw a number line on the whiteboard and label one end '0' and the other end '100'.

2. **Ask:** *Where do you think the number 50 would go?*

3. **Say:** *50 goes in the middle because it is halfway between 0 and 100.*

4. Repeat with 25 and 75 so that the pupils can see visual reference points for the rest of the task.

5. **Ask:** *Where would the number 90 go? How do you know this?*

6. Repeat with other numbers. Ask the pupils how they know a certain number goes in a certain place: 15 goes there because it is in between 0 and 25, etc.

7. Ask the pupils to draw their own number line and place the numbers 34, 56, 76 and 99 on it. You may want to encourage the pupils to place 50, 25 and 75 first to help.

Key checks: Are the pupils using clear reference points on the number line (half, quarter and three-quarter marks)? Are the pupils using the correct vocabulary: above, below, estimate, close to, about the same as, just over, just under?

Extension: Ask pupils to draw the following number lines: 0–100, 30–70 and 44–88. Ask them to place 44 on each number line and explain why they placed it there.

Support: Provide pupils with a strip of paper with blank intervals, 0–10. Pupils fold it in half and discuss how this shows half and is 5. Can the pupils fill in the missing numbers? Can they link this to a 100 number line?

Partitioning problems

Strand: Number – number and place value

Learning objective: To partition numbers in different ways.

You will need: Dienes, Numicon or Lego, whiteboard, whiteboard pen, board rubber

1. **Say:** *I'm going to need your help this lesson.*

2. Place a whiteboard flat on the table. Write the number 24 on the whiteboard. Place the Dienes/Numicon/Lego on the whiteboard incorrectly (to show incorrect representation), e.g. 2 tens and 3 ones.

3. **Ask:** *Is this correct? Why not?*

4. Encourage the pupils to explain their thoughts. (Steer their thoughts to there not being enough ones.)

5. Write this out: 24 = 20 + 4. Or:

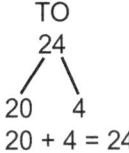

20 + 4 = 24

6. **Ask:** *Is there another way to partition 24?* (If the pupils don't know, write down 10 + 14.)

7. As a group, partition the number 46 using 4 tens and 6 ones.

8. **Ask:** *How could we write this down?* (40 + 6, 20 + 26 or 30 + 16)

9. Tell the pupils to create incorrect representations for a partner to correct (just like the first example).

10. As a final 'test', create an incorrect partition and see if the pupils agree with what you have done.

Key checks: Can the pupils explain their thinking by recording or demonstrating understanding? Are the pupils using the correct vocabulary: partition, recombine, tens, ones, separate, together?

Extension: Ask the pupils to complete problems such as: In the number 34 there are ___ tens and ___ ones.

Support: Pupils partition smaller two-digit numbers, e.g. 12: 1 ten and 2 ones.

Inequalities

Strand: Number – number and place value

Learning objectives: To compare and order numbers from 0 up to 100; to use <, > and = signs.

You will need: whiteboard, whiteboard pen, board rubber, cubes/Dienes/ multi-based arithmetic blocks

1. **Say:** *Today we will be learning how to compare numbers.*

2. Write the numbers 12 and 23 on the whiteboard.

3. **Ask:** *Which is the biggest number? How do you know? Can you show me how you know?* The pupils may use a drawing or some of the hands-on equipment suggested above.

4. Introduce 'inequalities' to the pupils. As a group, use Dienes equipment so that they can see a physical representation of the numbers to compare. Show 12 < 23 and 23 > 12.

5. Write 12 < 23 on the whiteboard.

6. **Say:** *This means 12 is less than 23.*

7. Go through several other examples using the symbols <, > and =.

8. Write 10 and 9 + 1 on the whiteboard.

9. **Ask:** *What symbol would we use for this?* (The pupils should answer = symbol.)

10. **Ask:** *Why? How do you know?* Discuss when we use the = symbol.

Key checks: Do pupils fully understand what the symbols represent (is more than, is less than, is equal to)? Are the pupils using the correct vocabulary: is more than, is less than, is equal to, more, less, smaller, greater, lesser, equal?

Extension: Write 7 + 2 and 9 – 0 and **ask:** *What symbol could we use here?* Encourage the pupils to create their own balancing equations using the = symbol.

Support: Allow pupils to work with numbers that are significantly larger/smaller and use concrete materials to show this, e.g. cubes.

Complicated counting

Strand: Number – number and place value

Learning objectives: To count in steps of 2, 3, and 5 from 0, and in tens from any number.

You will need: laminated 100 square (one per pupil), number lines, whiteboard, whiteboard pen, board rubber

1. Write the number 14 on the whiteboard.

2. **Ask:** *Can we count on in twos to this number?*

3. As a group, count in twos from 2 (4, 6, 8, 10, 12, 14) so that the pupils are used to counting in twos. Then move on to 16, 18, 20, 22, 24, etc.

4. Ask the pupils to show you this on their 100 square.

5. **Ask:** *Can you see a pattern when counting in twos on a 100 square?*

6. Repeat with count on in fives from to 5 to 25 and then from 25, 30, 35, 40, 45, 50 etc.

7. **Ask:** *Can you see a pattern when counting in fives on a 100 square?*

8. Repeat with counting in tens from 14: 14, 24, 34, 44, etc.

9. **Ask:** *Can you see a pattern when counting in tens on a 100 square?*

10. Repeat with counting in threes from 3, 6, 9, 12, 15, 18, 21, etc.

11. **Ask:** *Can you see a pattern when counting in threes on a 100 square?*

12. Repeat the activity a few times to allow the pupils to see the pattern.

Key checks: Before you start the activity, ensure that the pupils have some understanding of counting in twos, threes, fives and tens. Are the pupils using the correct vocabulary: count in twos, fives and tens, forwards from/backwards from, once, twice, three times, five times?

Extension: Can the pupils count in tens from any number without a 100 square?

Support: Provide the pupils with a number line as well as a 100 square to help them count independently. Pupils to show jumps with whiteboard pens working with smaller numbers starting from 0.

Code cracker

Strand: Number – number and place value

Learning objective: To use place value and number facts to solve problems.

You will need: whiteboards, whiteboard pens, board rubbers, Numicon or other practical equipment

1. Draw symbols at the top of the whiteboard such as:

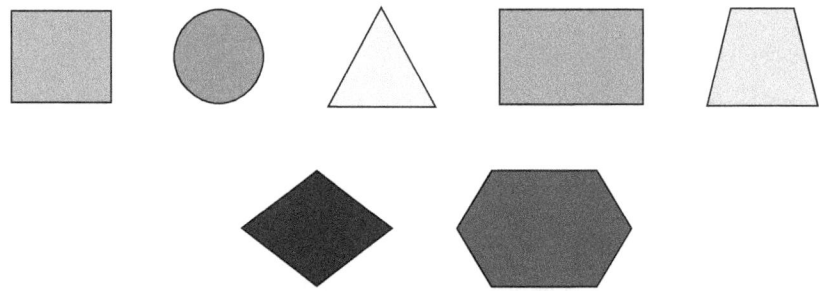

2. Write ▢ + ◆ = 9. **Ask:** *What could the value of the symbols be in this number sentence?* Allow pupils time to respond (e.g. 8 + 1 or 7 + 2).

3. **Ask:** *How do you know that these could be their value? Can you show me using the apparatus?*

4. Repeat this activity by putting another two symbols together on the board and asking the pupils to write the possible values of the symbols on their whiteboards.

Key checks: Are the pupils able to see the link between symbols and numbers? Are the pupils using the correct vocabulary: value, add, more, plus, make, sum, total, altogether, subtract, take away, minus?

Extension: Pupils create their own 'code' to crack and generate questions for each other.

Support: Pupils focus on problems that involve number bonds to 20 to build confidence before they move on.

Even Steven and Odd Todd

Strand: Number – number and place value

Learning objective: To be able to recognise odd and even numbers.

You will need: non-laminated 100 square (one per pupil) and cubes, different coloured pencils (enough for each pupil to have two colours of pencil each)

1. **Say:** *Today I am going to introduce you to two friends of mine: Even Steven and Odd Todd. Even Steven really likes even numbers and Odd Todd has an odd obsession with odd numbers and they both have a rhyme to help us remember the even and odd numbers. This can sometimes be tricky!*

2. **Say:** *Even numbers can be grouped in twos with none left over. Odd numbers will always have one left over if grouped in twos.* (You may wish to show this with cubes.)

3. **Say:** *Odd Todd likes to say 1, 3, 5, 7, 9, odd numbers are all fine!'*

4. Repeat this song several times.

5. **Say:** *Even Steven likes to say 0, 2, 4, 6, 8, even numbers are all great!*

6. Repeat this song several times.

7. Show the pupils a 100 square and ask them to colour the odd numbers one colour and the even numbers another colour.

8. After they have done this, **ask:** *What do you notice about the ones digits of the odd and even numbers?* (The ones digits in odd numbers are 1, 3, 5, 7 and 9 and the ones digits in even numbers are 0, 2, 4, 6 and 8.)

Key checks: Can the pupils remember the rhyme to help them? Are the pupils using the correct vocabulary: odd, even, same, similar, different?

Extension: Write down several numbers and ask the pupils to say if they are odd or even and why (e.g. 223, 547, 555, 809, 888).

Support: Pupils organise the numbers 0–9 into odd and even groups using cubes to represent each number (pupils to put the cubes together in pairs to clearly show odd and even numbers). Pupils to refer to this when answering questions.

Triple addition

Strand: Number – addition and subtraction

Learning objective: To add three one-digit numbers.

You will need: whiteboards, whiteboard pens, board rubbers, cubes, dice (0–9 and 0–6), number lines

1. **Ask:** *Who can add two numbers together using the equipment on the table?*

2. Write 4 + 5 = _____ on the whiteboard.

3. Encourage the pupils to use the equipment on the table to show you the answer.

4. Write: 4 + 5 = 9 on the whiteboard.

5. **Ask:** *Who thinks they could add three numbers together?*

6. Roll three dice and generate three numbers, e.g. 2, 5 and 7.

7. Using cubes, add the numbers together:

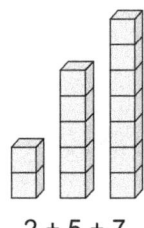

2 + 5 + 7

8. Ensure that you discuss getting to 10. **Say:** 2 + 5 = 7, then count on from 7 to 10. There are four left. 10 + 4 = 14. So 2 + 5 + 7 = 14. You may want to discuss doubles here (7 + 7).

9. Repeat this activity with different numbers and allow pupils to build their confidence.

___

Key checks: Can the pupils see the link between the cubes and the numbers? Are the pupils using the correct vocabulary: add, more, plus, make, sum, total, altogether, equals, together, doubles, near doubles?

Extension: Say: *Three numbers add up to 10. What could they be?* Pupils use equipment as well as number sentences to show their thinking.

Support: Allow pupils to work with smaller numbers first, e.g. 2 + 3 + 4, and don't go through the tens barrier until they are confident.

Bond pairs

Strand: Number – addition and subtraction

Learning objective: To know addition bonds of multiples of 10 for 100.

You will need: 0–9 die, Dienes, Numicon or Lego, 100 squares (one per pupil), number line, cards with multiples of 10 (10, 20, 30, 40, 50, 60, 70, 80, 90, 100)

1. **Say:** *Today we are going to explore number bonds to 10.* Roll a 0–9 die and **ask:** *What number needs to be added to make 10?* (e.g. roll a 6, 4 is needed to make 10) Repeat a few times.

2. Show the jumps on a number line or a 100 square. **Ask:** *Can you find 90 on your 100 square/number line?* Pupils point to the number. **Ask:** *How many jumps from 90 to 100?* Pupils show you a jump of 10. This could be 10 individual jumps of 1 or one big jump of 10.

3. **Say:** *When we count in multiples of 10 using a 100 square, one jump equals 10.*

4. As a group, clap out 1–100. Every time you say a multiple of 10, pupils 'spring' into the air and point at the correct 100 square.

5. As a group, count in tens, jumping each time and pointing at the correct 100 square to show this.

6. Show the pile of cards and turn one over (e.g. 80). **Ask:** *From what we know about number bonds to 10, what do you think we would need to add to 80 to make 100?* (20)

7. Show 8 + 2 using Dienes equipment and then repeat this showing 80 + 20, making sure the pupils see the link between the two.

8. Lay out all the cards and ask pupils to take turns to match a pair, e.g. turn one card over (30) and try to find the matching card (70).

Key checks: Do the pupils understand why they are clapping or jumping to represent the multiples of 10? Are the pupils using the correct vocabulary: number bond, pairs, add, together, multiple?

Extension: Provide pupils with a number sentence, e.g. 60 + ? = 100, and ask them to explain their reasoning for the answer.

Support: Pupils concentrate on number bonds to 10 before they move onto bonds to 100. Pupils show the link between all number bonds to 10 and 100 by using the equipment provided.

Subtraction pairs

Strand: Number – addition and subtraction

Learning objective: To know subtraction bonds of multiples of 10 for 100.

You will need: Dienes, Numicon or Lego, 100 square, number line, cards with multiples of 10 (10, 20, 30, 40, 50, 60, 70, 80, 90, 100)

1. Show the pupils the pile of cards, then turn one over, e.g. 30.

2. **Ask:** *100 – 30, what number bond to 10 does that remind you of?* (10 – 3) You may wish to show the pupils this using ten sticks and cubes.

3. **Say:** *10 take away 3 is 7 and 100 take away 30 is 70.*

4. **Say:** *If we know 100 – 30 is 70, what is 100 – 70?* (30). You will need to show the process with base 10 apparatus, pointing out the bonds between the numbers.

5. Repeat this activity with another card.

6. Lay out all the cards and ask pupils to take it in turns to match a pair, e.g. they turn one card over (60) and try to find the matching card (40).

7. Repeat this activity to consolidate learning.

Key checks: Can the pupils show explanation using the 100 square? Are the pupils using the correct vocabulary: number bonds, take away, subtract, minus, 10 less, less?

Extension: If the number is 50 or above, the pupils should count up to find the answer, e.g. 100 – 60, count from 60 upwards for a speedy answer. Ask the pupils to solve questions such as 80 + ? = 100 and 100 – ? = 70.

Support: Pupils concentrate on subtraction bonds to 10 before they move onto subtraction bonds to 100. Pupils show the link between all subtraction bonds to 10 and 100 by using equipment provided.

Awesome addition

Strand: Number – addition and subtraction

Learning objective: To be able to add a two-digit number and ones.

You will need: whiteboards, whiteboard pens, 0–6 and 0–9 dice, base 10 equipment

1. **Say:** *Today we are going to learn more about addition.*

2. **Ask:** *What is addition?*

3. **Say:** *Addition is finding the sum, or total, by joining two or more numbers together.*

4. **Say:** *Today we will be adding a one-digit number to a two-digit number.*

5. **Ask:** *Can anyone show me a one-digit number on their board?* Pupils write/ draw/use equipment to show a one-digit number.

6. **Ask:** *Can anyone show me a two-digit number on their board?* Pupils write/ draw/use equipment to show a two-digit number.

7. Write 41 on the board and roll a 0–6 die, e.g. it might land on 3.

8. **Ask:** *What is 41 add 3?* Pupils to respond.

9. **Ask:** *How do you know? Can you show me on your board?*

10. Draw a number line on the whiteboard and show the pupils 41 + 3 by counting on.

11. Count on together. **Say:** *42, 43, 44: 41 add 3 equals 44.*

12. Repeat this activity with different numbers without crossing over the tens barrier.

13. Ask pupils to investigate what happens when we add into the next 10, e.g. 28 + 3. **Say:** *We exchange 10 ones for a ten and have 3 tens and 1 one.* (Show this using equipment.)

Key checks: Can the pupils explain their thinking and verbalise how they know the answer? Are the pupils using the correct vocabulary: add, more, plus, make, sum, total, altogether, equals?

Extension: Give the pupils numbers close to the tens barrier and a 0–9 die, e.g. 57 + 8 = 65.

Support: Provide the pupils with a 100 square/number line filled in to help them count on. Do not cross over the tens barrier until confident, e.g. 36 + 3 = 39 followed by 49 + 4 = 53.

Dicey subtraction

Strand: Number – addition and subtraction

Learning objective: To be able to subtract a two-digit number and ones.

You will need: whiteboards, whiteboard pens, board rubbers, 0–6 and 0–9 dice, base 10 equipment

1. **Say:** *Today we are going to learn more about subtraction.*

2. **Ask:** *What is subtraction?*

3. **Say:** *One example of subtraction is take away.*

4. **Say:** *Today we will be subtracting a one-digit number from a two-digit number.*

5. Write the number 68 and draw a number line on the whiteboard. Show this using base 10 equipment.

6. Roll a 0–6 die to generate a number to take away, e.g. 5.

7. **Ask:** *What is 68 subtract 5?*

8. **Ask:** *How do you know? Can you show me on your board?*

9. Explain that we can count backwards using a number line or take away using apparatus.

10. Write 68 at the end of a number line and, as a group, draw the jumps backwards as you subtract.

11. Count backwards together. **Say:** *67, 66, 65, 64, 63. 68 subtract 5 equals 63.*

12. Repeat this activity with different numbers without crossing over the tens barrier.

13. Ask pupils to investigate what happens when we subtract into the previous 10, e.g. 23 – 5. **Say:** *We exchange one of our tens for 10 ones.* Can the pupils show this using equipment?

Key checks: Can the pupils explain their thinking and verbalise how they know the answer? Are the pupils using the correct vocabulary: subtract, take away, minus, difference, equals?

Extension: Give the pupils numbers close to the tens barrier and a 0–9 die, e.g. 71 – 8 = 63.

Support: Provide each pupil with a 100 square/number line filled in to help them count back. Do not cross over the tens barrier until confident, e.g. 43 – 3 = 40 followed by 43 – 5 = 38.

100 square addition

Strand: Number – addition and subtraction

Learning objective: To be able to add a two-digit number and tens.

You will need: 100 squares (one for each pupil), number cards (multiples of 10: 10, 20, 30, 40, 50, 60, 70, 80, 90), number lines, base 10 apparatus

1. **Ask:** *Who is good at counting in tens?*
2. As a group, chant the 10 multiplication table together up to 120.
3. **Ask:** *Can you count in tens from 1?*
4. Give the pupils time to respond.
5. On a 100 square, highlight 1.
6. **Ask:** *How can we count in tens using the 100 square?*
7. **Say:** *We can count in tens all the way down through the 100 square.*
8. As a group, highlight and count 1, 11, 21, 31, 41, 51, 61, 71, 81, 91.
9. Highlight the number 34 and choose a number card, e.g. 30.
10. **Ask:** *What is 34 add 30? How many jumps of 10 do we need to make? Which way do we jump? Why?*
11. Model 34 + 30 using base 10 apparatus.
12. As a group, count on 3 tens from 34. **Say:** *44, 54, 64. 34 add 30 equals 64.*
13. Repeat with other numbers.
14. When pupils become confident, allow them to do this activity independently.

Key checks: Do the pupils understand which way to jump when adding? Can they explain why they jump that way? (In this case numbers are getting larger by tens.) Are the pupils using the correct vocabulary: add, more, plus, make, sum, total, altogether, equals, tens digit?

Extension: Ask pupils to use a number line to show you the jumps of 10.

Support: Provide the pupils with a 100 square and focus on adding 10, 20 and 30 or use Dienes equipment to show adding tens to the original number.

100 square subtraction

Strand: Number – addition and subtraction

Learning objective: To be able to subtract a two-digit number and tens.

You will need: 100 squares (one for each pupil), number lines, number cards (multiples of tens: 10, 20, 30, 40, 50, 60, 70, 80, 90), Dienes equipment

1. **Ask:** *Who is good at counting backwards in tens?* Highlight the number 100 on the 100 square and, as a group, count backwards. **Say:** 100, 90, 80, 70, 60, ..., 0.

2. **Ask:** *How can we count backwards in tens using the 100 square?*

3. On a 100 square, highlight 98. **Say:** *We can count backwards in tens from 98 by looking up the column that 98 is placed in.* Can the pupils see the connection between 98, 88, 78, etc.?

4. As a group, highlight and count 98, 88, 78, 68, 58, 48, 38, 28, 18, 8.

5. **Ask:** *Which operation is counting backwards like?* **Say:** *Counting backwards is just like subtracting because the numbers are getting smaller.*

6. Highlight the number 84 and choose a number card, e.g. 20.

7. **Ask:** *What is 84 subtract 20? How many jumps of 10 do we need to make? Which way do we jump? Why?*

8. As a group, count back 2 tens from 84. **Say:** *84 to 74, 74 to 64. 84 subtract 20 equals 64.*

9. Repeat with other numbers.

10. When the pupils become confident, allow them to do this activity independently.

Key checks: Do the pupils understand which way to jump when subtracting? Can they explain why? (In this case the tens digit is getting smaller.) Are the pupils using the correct vocabulary: subtract, take away, minus, difference, count on, count back, tens digit?

Extension: Can the pupils use a number line to show you the jumps of 10?

Support: Pupils count back in tens from 90 to begin with. Can they identify the pattern and apply this to 99? (the tens digit changes, but the ones digit does not) Focus on subtracting 10, 20 and 30 or use Dienes equipment to show adding tens to the original number.

Is it possible?

Strand: Number – addition and subtraction

Learning objective: To be able to show that addition of two numbers can be done in any order (commutative) and subtraction of one number from another cannot.

You will need: whiteboards, whiteboard pens, board rubbers, number lines, cubes

1. **Ask:** *Who can add and subtract?* **Say:** *Today we will be learning more about how addition and subtraction are different. Addition is a story that can be told any way to get the same ending.*

2. Write 5 + 3 = _____ and 3 + 5 = _____ on the whiteboard.

3. **Ask:** *What is 5 + 3?* (8) *What is 3 + 5?* (8)

4. Draw a number line and show both number stories using equipment, e.g. cubes.

5. **Say:** *Unlike addition, subtraction is a story that can only be told one way to get the same ending.* Write 9 – 4 = _____ and 4 – 9 = _____ on the whiteboard.

6. **Ask:** *What is 9 – 4?* (5) *What is 4 – 9?* (Note that this goes beyond zero and Year 2 pupils do not need to know it. Complete these calculations using cubes so pupils can see that they cannot physically complete 4 – 9.)

7. Repeat with different simple questions.

8. Check understanding by writing two questions and asking which can be done in any order, e.g. 9 + 8 = (yes) and 8 – 5 = (no).

Key checks: Do the pupils know what happens if we subtract a bigger number from a smaller number? (negatives). Do the pupils understand to add when they see the + symbol and subtract when they see the – symbol? Are the pupils using the correct vocabulary: add, more, plus, make, sum, total, altogether, equals, subtract, take away, minus, difference?

Extension: Pupils use a bar model to explore the relationship between addition and subtraction facts. Pupils to investigate the four possible answers (29 = 14 + 15, 29 = 15 + 14, 29 – 14 = 15, 29 – 15 = 14).

29	
14	15

Support: Pupils work with smaller numbers to build confidence (e.g. 4 + 3 = 7 and 3 – 4 = not possible with apparatus). Refer to a number line to demonstrate process.

Shopaholics

Strand: Number – addition and subtraction

Learning objectives: To use concrete objects and pictorial representations to solve addition and subtraction problems. To solve simple problems in a practical context involving addition and subtraction of money of the same unit, including giving change.

You will need: whiteboard, whiteboard pen, board rubber, number lines, cubes, money (ideally real), a variety of objects to 'sell', each with a price tag, some of the price tags must add up to 50p, £1, 20p and 10p

1. **Ask:** *Who has paid for something before? What do we use to pay for shopping?* (Stay away from use of cards and concentrate on money.)

2. **Say:** *Today we will be buying objects from the Year 2 shop.* Warm up by finding the correct money to pay for a single item, then move on to paying too much. Identify the calculation needed to work out the change and then solve it.

3. Pick up two objects that add up to 20p. **Ask:** *What is the total price of these two items?* (20p)

4. Pick up an object worth 10p. **Say:** *Let's see if we can work out a problem using bar modelling.*

5. **Say:** *If I pay for this 10p item with a 20p* (draw a bar model of this showing 20p), *how much change will I get?* (draw a bar underneath showing 10p) *We could use cubes or a number line to count on to find the difference.* (10p)

20p	
10p	

6. Repeat with several different combinations.

7. Pupils take turns to be the shopkeeper and give change.

Key checks: Can the pupils tell you the value of each coin? Are the pupils using the correct vocabulary: money, coin, pence, pound, price, cost, buy, sell, spend, spent, pay, change, dear(er), costs more, costs less, cheaper, costs the same as, add, subtract, take away, together, altogether, total?

Extension: Pupils buy three or four objects to test addition and subtraction skills.

Support: Provide pupils with a number line to support addition and subtraction strategies. Focus on one-step problems and giving change with 1p coins. Then explore how 1 pence coins make up other amounts.

Counting on

Strand: Number – multiplication and division

Learning objective: To recall and use multiplication and division facts for the 2, 3 and 5 multiplication tables.

You will need: whiteboard, whiteboard pen, board rubber, number line, 100 square

1. **Say:** *Today we will be counting in twos, threes and fives.*

2. **Ask:** *Can you count in twos, threes and fives already?*

3. Show the pupils a 100 square and, as a group, count through the twos, threes and fives together up to 12 × 2/3/5.

4. Once you have established that the pupils can count in twos, threes and fives, move on to the next step.

5. **Say:** *Now we are going to count in twos, threes and fives from different numbers.*

6. Write 15 on the whiteboard.

7. **Ask:** *Can you count in threes from this number? What would the next number be?* The pupils should respond with the answer of 18. If not, show this on a number line and count on 3 together as a group.

8. Count together as a group and add on 3 each time: *18, 21, 24, 27, 30, 33.*

9. Repeat with other numbers, e.g. 25: count in fives, 18: count in twos, 33: count in threes.

Key checks: Can the pupils count in twos, threes and fives already? Are the pupils using the correct vocabulary: add on, count on from, product, multiple of, times, multiply, multiply by?

Extension: Pupils count on from more challenging numbers, e.g. count on in threes from 66, and count back in twos, threes and fives.

Support: Pupils count on in fives to begin with to build confidence. Then move on to twos and threes when confident.

Missing symbols

Strand: Number – multiplication and division

Learning objective: To calculate mathematical statements for multiplication and division within the multiplication tables and write them using the multiplication (×), division (÷) and equals (=) signs.

You will need: cubes/counters, whiteboards, whiteboard pens, board rubbers

1. **Ask:** *What is multiplication?* Allow pupils time to respond. **Say:** *One way of looking at multiplication is that it is repeated addition.*

2. **Ask:** *What is division?* Allow pupils time to respond. **Say:** *One way of looking at division is that it is splitting numbers of objects into equal groups or fair sharing, or even repeated subtraction.*

3. As a group, complete several multiplication and division questions to ensure the pupils gain a clear understanding of multiplication and division. Encourage them to make arrays when multiplying and dividing using cubes.

4. Write 4 _____ 2 = 8 and **ask:** *Which symbol is missing from this number sentence?* (the × symbol). *How do you know that? Why is it not the + or the – symbol? Show me using the materials on the table.*

5. Write 2 = 10 _____ 5 and **ask:** *What is missing from this number sentence?* (÷) *Why is it not ×, + or –? Explain your answer using the equipment on the table.*

6. Repeat for a number of these types of questions, e.g. 3 ___ 5 = 15, 5 = 1 ___ 5.

Key checks: Do the pupils have an understanding of multiplication and division prior to commencing this task? If you show an array for multiplication or division and you ask the pupils to write down if it is multiplication or division, can they do it? Are the pupils using the correct vocabulary: multiple of, lots of, times, multiply, multiply by, divide, divided by, groups of, product, equals, sum of, answer?

Extension: Draw an array showing 20 (2 columns of 10) and **ask:** *Can you write any other multiplication or addition facts that this array shows? Can you write one division fact?*

Support: Consolidate knowledge of twos, fives and tens and focus on multiplication, then division. Use physical equipment to explore thinking. Pupils begin with repeated addition to show the calculation, e.g. 2 + 2 + 2 = 3 lots of 2 or 3 × 2 (show as an array with the equipment).

Sweet maths

Strand: Number – multiplication and division

Learning objectives: To solve problems involving multiplication and division, using materials, arrays, repeated addition, mental methods and multiplication and division facts, including problems in contexts.

You will need: a few packets of sweets (or use some cubes), whiteboards, whiteboard pens, board rubbers, number lines, 100 square, multiplication square

1. **Ask:** *Can you remember what multiplication and division are?* Remind them that one way of thinking about multiplication is that it is repeated addition and one way of thinking about division is that it is splitting numbers or objects into equal groups or fair sharing.

2. **Say:** *Today we will be showing multiplication and division using sweets!*

3. **Say:** *[Name of pupil 1], [name of pupil 2], [name of pupil 3] and [name of pupil 4] all have five sweets each* (give each pupil five sweets). *How many sweets do they have altogether?*

4. As a group, count the sweets in fives. **Say:** *5, 10, 15, 20. There are 20 sweets altogether.*

5. Model writing the number statement: 4 × 5 = 20.

6. **Say:** *I have 12 sweets and I am going to share them equally between 6 pupils. How many sweets will each pupil get?*

7. Share the sweets out evenly and count how many each pupil gets. (2)

8. Repeat with different multiplication tables (2, 5 and 10).

Key checks: Make sure that during step 3 the pupils hear you sharing the sweets out; emphasise the *equally shared* aspect. Make sure the pupils have a go at sharing the sweets to complete the calculations. Are the pupils using the correct vocabulary: multiple of, multiply, lots of, multiply by, divide, divided by, groups of, product, equals, answer, share, share equally, equal groups of, each?

Extension: Allow the pupils to share in harder multiplication tables (e.g. low 3 multiplication table). Pupils find different arrays to show the same answer, e.g. 10: 2 × 5 = 10, 5 × 2 = 10, 1 × 10 = 10, 10 × 1 = 10.

Support: Pupils draw boxes on their whiteboards to represent the divisor (dividing number), e.g. 12 sweets shared between 6, means 6 squares drawn on their board ready to place sweets/cubes in.

Total recall

Strand: Number – multiplication and division

Learning objective: To recall and use multiplication and division facts for the 2, 5 and 10 multiplication tables.

You will need: 100 square (one per pupil), counters/coloured pencils, coins, number lines

1. Show the pupils a 100 square grid. Colour in/place a counter on the 2 and 4.

2. **Ask:** *Does anyone know why I covered/coloured 2 and 4?* Listen to their answers.

3. **Ask:** *What do you think I will cover next?* Encourage the pupils to answer.

4. Ask the pupils to colour in/place a counter on the even numbers.

5. **Ask:** *What are we counting in?* (twos). *What do we notice about the 2 multiplication table?*

6. Ask the pupils to do the same for the 5 and 10 multiplication tables.

7. **Ask:** *Do you notice a pattern? What can you see?*

8. **Ask:** *What do you know from this?* i.e. 2 × 5 is _____.

9. Show the pupils a pile of 1p, 2p, 5p and 10p coins.

10. As a group, count the 1p coins to 12: *1, 2, 3, 4, 5, 6, 7, 8, 9, 10, 11, 12.* **Say:** *There are 12 1p coins here.*

11. Encourage the pupils to do the same with the 2p coins, 5p coins and 10p coins (count 12 of them).

Key checks: Can the pupils see the links between the twos, fives and tens? Are the pupils using the correct vocabulary: multiple of, multiply, multiply by?

Extension: Pupils write out known facts from this activity, e.g. 4 × 5 = 20 and 2 × 10 = 20.

Support: Provide pupils with a number line/100 square that is not covered to support counting.

Can we do it?

Strand: Number – multiplication and division

Learning objective: To show that multiplication of two numbers can be done in any order (commutative).

You will need: whiteboards, whiteboard pens, board rubbers, cubes

1. **Ask:** *What is 2 × 3?* (6) Explain that 2 + 2 + 2 is the same as 2 × 3.

2. **Ask:** *What is 3 × 2?* (6) Explain that 3 + 3 is the same as 3 × 2.

3. **Ask:** *What do you notice about these two calculations?* (They have the same amount/same product.)

4. Show 4 × 2 and 2 × 4 as arrays (cubes or drawn):

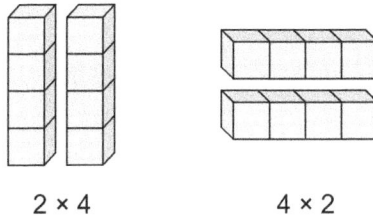

$$2 \times 4 \qquad\qquad 4 \times 2$$

5. Rotate the arrays to show the pupils they are the same representation.

6. **Ask:** *What can you tell me about these two calculations?* (They have the same amount/same product.) **Say:** *This shows us that multiplication can be done in any order, 4 × 2 or 2 × 4 gives us the same answer.*

7. Count in twos to find the answer:

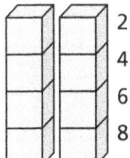 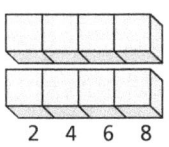

Continues

8. Write a variety of multiplication questions on the whiteboard and ask the pupils to see if what you have said is true, e.g. 3 × 4, 2 × 5, 6 × 10.

9. **Say:** *As you can see, the multiplication of two numbers can be done in any order.*

Key checks: Can the pupils see that the product is the same whichever way the array is arranged (horizontal or vertical)? Ensure that the pupils can use arrays, just as above, with twos, then fives and then tens. Focus on counting the horizontal cubes and then vertical cubes to write the multiplication statement. Then count up in the multiples to create the product, e.g. 2 across, 4 up equals 2 × 4. 2, 4, 6, 8. 2 × 4 = 8. Are the pupils using the correct vocabulary: multiple of, multiply, multiply by, array, row, and column?

Extension: Give the pupils harder multiplication questions within known multiplication tables, e.g. 8 × 5 or 9 × 10.

Support: Pupils to focus on the 2 multiplication table.

Dubious division

Strand: Number – multiplication and division

Learning objective: To show that multiplication of two numbers can be done in any order (commutative) and division of one number by another cannot.

You will need: counters or cubes, whiteboards, whiteboard pens, board rubbers

1. **Ask:** *What did you learn about multiplication in the previous lesson?* Pupils should say that two numbers can be multiplied in any order and still have the same answer. (For example, 4 × 2 or 2 × 4.)

2. **Ask:** *Is this true for division too? Does it matter which way round the numbers are when we divide?*

3. Write 8 ÷ 4 on the whiteboard. **Ask:** *Is 8 ÷ 4 the same as 4 ÷ 8? Let's find out!*

4. Show the pupils 8 cubes/counters and then share them between 4:

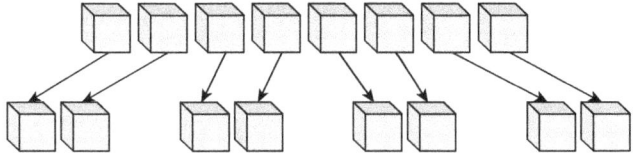

5. **Say:** *8 ÷ 4 = 2 because each group has 2 in it.*

6. Show 4 ÷ 8.

7. Once the four cubes have been shared, **say:** *There are four groups without anything!*

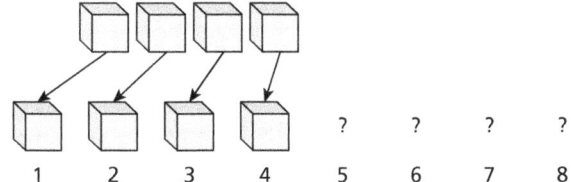

8. Show the pupils that each group would have a half:

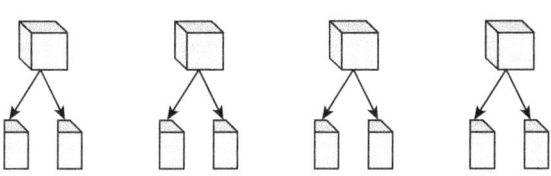

Continues

9. Repeat with several other calculations, e.g. 10 ÷ 5, 16 ÷ 2.

10. Encourage the pupils to attempt this independently to see what language they use.

Key checks: Do the pupils understand that division cannot be done in any order? Are the pupils using the correct vocabulary: divide, divided by, equals?

Extension: Pupils share out odd numbers, e.g. 9 divided by 3 = 3.

Support: Use cubes/counters to unpack the calculation. On a whiteboard, pupils draw squares to represent the divisor (dividing number) and place objects equally. Important to methodically place one object into each square at a time.

Contextual multiplication

Strand: Number – multiplication and division

Learning objective: To solve simple multiplication problems in a range of contexts (practically and pictorially).

You will need: whiteboards, whiteboard pens, board rubbers, cubes, number line, multiplication grids

1. **Say:** *Today we will learn more about multiplication.* **Ask:** *What is multiplication?*

2. Remind pupils that multiplication is repeated addition and grouping.

3. Write the following problem on the board: 5 friends had 2 sweets each. How many sweets did they have altogether? **Say:** *Highlight the important parts of the question.* (5 friends, 2 sweets each, how many, altogether)

4. **Say:** *We could use arrays to show our working out like this.*

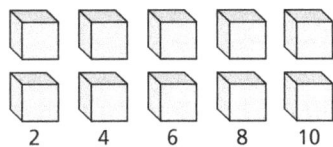

5. **Say:** *Or we could use a number line and count in twos like this.*

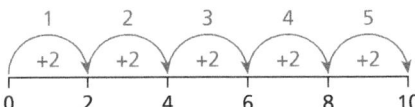

6. Repeat with more multiplication questions about the twos, fives and tens. Encourage pupils to solve the questions independently using both arrays and a number line, e.g. Jinda bought 5 eggs a week over an 8-week period. How many did she buy altogether? (5 × 8)

Key checks: Ensure that when you use the number line you talk about how each jump is one multiple and that multiplying is repeated addition. Can the pupils see the connections between arrays and a number line? Are the pupils using the correct vocabulary: multiple of, multiply, multiply by, array, row, altogether?

Extension: Allow the pupils to work with harder multiplication tables (e.g. the 3 multiplication table).

Support: Focus on creating the calculation from the information given. Can they identify which numbers to use? Can they use methods from previous learning?

Contextual multiplication and division

Strand: Number – multiplication and division

Learning objective: To solve simple multiplication and division problems in a range of contexts.

You will need: whiteboards, whiteboard pens, board rubbers, cubes, number lines

Note: Split over two sessions if necessary.

1. **Say:** *Today we will be learning more about multiplication and division.*
   Ask: *What is multiplication? What is division?*

2. Remind pupils that one way of thinking about multiplication is that it is repeated addition and one way to think about division is that it is splitting numbers or objects into equal groups or fair sharing.

3. Write the following problem on the board: There were 4 chefs who had 5 aprons each. How many aprons did they have altogether?

4. **Ask:** *Is this a multiplication problem or a division problem? How do we know?*

5. **Say:** *Highlight the important parts of the question. (4 chefs, 5 aprons each, how many, altogether)*

6. Go through the problem on the board using a number line:

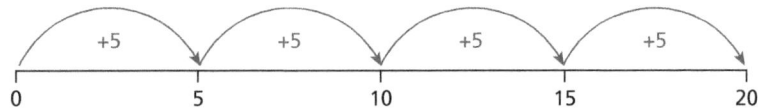

7. Write the following problem on the board: Misha, John, Hurshal, Aimee and Jeff share 15 sweets. How many sweets do they get each?

8. **Ask:** *Is this a multiplication problem or a division problem? How do we know?*

9. **Say:** *Highlight the important parts of the question. (5 friends, share, 15 sweets, how many, each)*

10. **Say:** *We could physically share by giving one sweet at a time to each person and we should end up with equal groups. We can show our working out like this:*

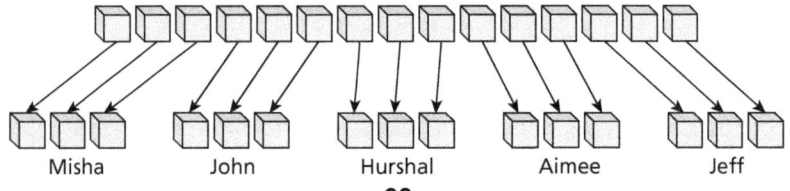

Misha   John   Hurshal   Aimee   Jeff

Continues

11. **Say:** *Or we could solve this problem on a number line using our multiplication facts, like this:*

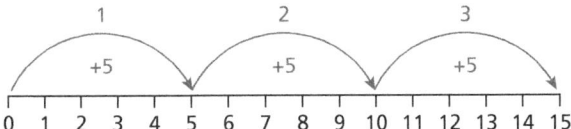

12. **Say:** *Or we could count back from 15 in fives, like this:*

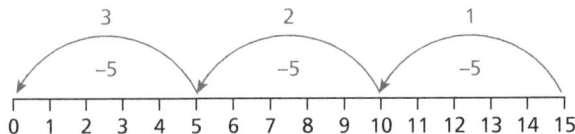

13. Use these methods to solve more word problems, e.g. There are 10 candles in a pack. Jo needs 40 candles. How many packs does Jo need altogether? (4) Freddy and Jack share a bag of 24 marbles. How many do they get each? (12) 10 friends went to a party. 40 balloons were shared equally for a game. How many balloons did each friend receive? (4)

Key checks: Can the pupils identify if the question is multiplication or division? Ensure that when you use the number line you talk about how each jump is one multiple or group and that multiplying is repeated addition of groups. Discuss counting backwards for the division method. Can the pupils see the connections between arrays and a number line? Are the pupils using the correct vocabulary: multiple of, multiply, multiply by, divide, divided by, product, equals, altogether, each?

Extension: Allow the pupils to work with harder multiplication tables.

Support: Focus on the pupils creating the calculation from the information given. Can they identify which numbers to use? Can they use the methods from previous learning (i.e. sharing)?

Chocolate conundrum 1

Strand: Number – fractions

Learning objective: To count in fractions (halves) up to 10.

You will need: fraction bars (e.g. chocolate bars), whiteboards, whiteboard pens, board rubbers

1. **Ask:** *Who likes chocolate?*

2. **Ask:** *What happens when we have to share a chocolate bar?*

3. **Say:** *When we share, we try to share equally so that each person gets the same amount of chocolate and the sharing is fair.*

4. Show the pupils one chocolate bar and **ask:** *How much chocolate would two people get if they shared it equally?* (The pupils may respond with half of the number of squares the bar contains, e.g. 6 if there are 12 squares each, or they might say 'half'.)

5. Draw a line or cut the chocolate bar in half and **say:** *Each person would get half.*

6. **Ask:** *How many halves are there in three chocolate bars?*

7. As a group, draw a line/cut the three chocolate bars into halves. Make sure that the pupils draw this on their whiteboards and write down $\frac{1}{2}$ above each half of the chocolate bar.

8. **Say:** *There are six halves in three whole chocolate bars.*

9. Repeat this activity with six, nine and 10 chocolate bars.

Key checks: Do the pupils understand that division is fair sharing/each person gets an equal/same amount? Are the pupils using the correct vocabulary: whole, equal parts, one half, two halves?

Extension: Pupils could use the knowledge from this task and draw out how many halves would be in seven or eight chocolate bars (pupils may be able to apply knowledge of near doubles for this).

Support: Pupils to concentrate on finding half of smaller numbers.

Chocolate conundrum 2

Strand: Number – fractions

Learning objective: To count in fractions (quarters) up to 10.

You will need: 10 fraction bars (e.g. chocolate bars), whiteboards, whiteboard pens, board rubbers

1. Recap what a half is. **Ask:** *How many halves are there in one whole chocolate bar?* Make sure pupils understand what a half is.

2. Draw a 'chocolate bar' on the whiteboard and split it into four pieces.

3. **Ask:** *If four people share a chocolate bar, how much does each person get?*

4. **Say:** *Each person gets one of the four pieces. This can be written as* $\frac{1}{4}$. (Write this on the board.) Show this with a chocolate bar and cut it into quarters.

5. Show two chocolate bars and **ask:** *How much chocolate would four people get if they shared two bars equally?* (two equal pieces each)

6. Draw a line or cut the chocolate bars in quarters and **say:** *Each person would have a quarter each.*

7. **Ask:** *How many quarters are there in five chocolate bars?*

8. As a group, draw a line/cut the five chocolate bars into quarters. Make sure the pupils draw this on their whiteboards and write $\frac{1}{4}$ above each quarter of the chocolate bars. **Say:** *There are 20 quarters in five whole chocolate bars.*

9. Draw a number line from 0–5 and, as a group, mark where the quarters go $(0, \frac{1}{4}, \frac{2}{4}, \frac{3}{4}, 1, 1\frac{1}{4}, 1\frac{2}{4}, 1\frac{3}{4}, 2$ etc.).

10. Repeat with three chocolate bars, eight chocolate bars and 10 chocolate bars.

Key checks: Do the pupils understand that there are four quarters in a whole? Are the pupils using the correct vocabulary: whole, equal parts, four equal parts, one quarter, two quarters?

Extension: Pupils work out how many quarters would be in six, seven or nine chocolate bars (they may apply knowledge of doubling for this).

Support: Consolidate knowledge of a half before moving on to quarters. Provide pupils with the cut quarters so that they can physically manipulate them to see how many quarters are in the given number of chocolate bars.

Fraction number line

Strand: Number – fractions

Learning objective: To position fractions on a number line.

You will need: whiteboards, whiteboard pens, board rubbers, plastic fraction circles (or handmade versions of 1 whole, halves and quarters), paper

1. Draw $\frac{1}{4}, \frac{1}{2}, \frac{3}{4}$ and 1 as circles and squares on the whiteboard or use plastic fraction circles as a visual aid.

2. **Ask:** *What are these?* (fractions/parts of a whole) *Can you name these fractions?* Give pupils time to name and label the fractions.

3. Wipe the board clean and then write down $\frac{1}{4}, \frac{1}{2}, \frac{3}{4}$ and 1.

4. Point to one at a time and ask the pupils to draw an image of them on their boards

5. Ensure the pupils can associate the written fraction with the drawn fraction.

6. Draw a number line on the board from 0 to 1.

7. **Ask:** *Where does $\frac{1}{2}$ go on this number line? How do we know? Can you prove it?* As a group, place $\frac{1}{2}$ on the number line.

8. **Ask:** *Which fraction should we place on the number line next?* Encourage the pupils to choose which fraction goes on next, but remember to ask why they have chosen that fraction and their reasons for this.

9. As a group, place all the fractions on the whiteboard.

10. Ask the pupils to draw their own number line and then draw an image of each fraction in the correct place. After this, they can label each one ($\frac{1}{4}, \frac{1}{2}, \frac{3}{4}$ and 1 whole).

11. Draw a number line 0–10 and, as a group, write where the $\frac{1}{2}$ (halves) go, then the $\frac{1}{4}$ (quarters) and the $\frac{3}{4}$ (three-quarters).

Key checks: Do the pupils understand the symbol for each fraction and can they draw each shape to match? Are the pupils using the correct vocabulary: whole, equal parts, four equal parts, one half, two halves, a quarter, two quarters, three quarters?

Extension: Pupils find $\frac{1}{4}$ of numbers to 20.

Support: Give the pupils a strip of paper. Fold in half. **Ask:** *What can you tell me?* Fold again. **Ask:** *What do you see?* Cut the strip into quarters. Piece back together and build the fraction strip labelling $\frac{1}{4}, \frac{1}{2}, \frac{3}{4}$, 1.

Fractions of...

Strand: Number – fractions

Learning objective: To find $\frac{1}{4}$, $\frac{1}{2}$ and $\frac{3}{4}$ of quantities.

You will need: cubes, whiteboards, whiteboard pens, board rubbers

1. Recap a half and a quarter. Ask pupils to draw a circle or a square on their whiteboards. **Ask:** *Can you show me a half/quarter?*

2. Ask the pupils to split their whiteboard into four quarters. **Ask:** *Can you show me one quarter.* **Ask:** *If we shade two sections, how many quarters do we have? Can you show me three-quarters on your whiteboards?*

3. **Say:** *In this session, you will be looking at finding half, quarter or three-quarters of an amount/quantity.*

4. Show the pupils 20 cubes and **ask:** *How can I find a quarter of these cubes?*

5. Give the pupils time to answer; if nobody responds, **say:** *We can put them into four groups to show quarters.*

6. Show the pupils how to split the 20 cubes by putting one cube at a time into each quarter of a whiteboard until there are five cubes in each quarter. **Say:** *One quarter of 20 is 5 or 5 is one quarter of 20.*

7. **Ask:** *Can we find three-quarters of 20 if we know that one quarter is 5?*

8. Explain that they can count three sections of their boards. **Say:** *5, 10, 15. Three-quarters of 20 is 15.*

9. **Ask:** *Can we find out what half of 20 is?* Go through half with the group.

10. Repeat this process as a group with different numbers of cubes.

11. Allow the pupils time to answer further problems independently and take note of who can use the above strategy.

Key checks: Ensure pupils understand what each fraction is before they find fractions of quantities. Are the pupils using the correct vocabulary: whole, equal parts, four equal parts, one half, two halves, a quarter, two quarters, three quarters?

Extension: See if the pupils can see the link between $\frac{2}{4}$ and $\frac{1}{2}$. Can they apply what they have learnt to finding $\frac{1}{3}$ of a quantity?

Support: Allow the pupils to find a half and quarter of simple numbers to begin with (4, 8, 12, 16) to build their confidence.

Who gets more?

Strand: Number – fractions

Learning objective: To find equivalent fractions.

You will need: several fraction bars (e.g. chocolate bars), whiteboard, whiteboard pen, board rubber, fraction shapes

1. **Say:** *Today we will find out who gets the largest fraction of a chocolate bar.*

2. Verbally give each pupil a different fraction of a chocolate bar, e.g. $\frac{1}{4}, \frac{1}{2}, \frac{3}{4}, \frac{2}{4}$, $\frac{4}{4}$ or 1 whole.

3. Give each pupil a fraction bar and ask them to shade or cut a strip to show their fraction of the chocolate bar.

4. **Ask:** *Who will get the largest fraction of the chocolate bar? How do we know this? Can we stand in order to show this?* At this point, the pupils should see that the people with $\frac{2}{4}$ and those with a half have the same amount as do the people with $\frac{4}{4}$ and 1 whole. If not, you will need to point this out to them.

5. **Ask:** *Does anyone have the same fraction of the chocolate bar as someone else?*

6. Give the pupils time to see who has the same amount as them.

7. **Ask:** *What can we say about these fractions?* Give pupils time to say what they are thinking.

8. Write on the whiteboard as a group that $\frac{1}{2} = \frac{2}{4}$ and 1 whole $= \frac{4}{4}$.

9. **Ask:** *Can we find any other fractions that are the same?* ($\frac{2}{2}$ and 1 whole)

10. **Say:** *When fractions are the same we call them 'equivalent'.*

Key checks: Can pupils see that $\frac{2}{4}$ is the same as $\frac{1}{2}$? Can they find any other half fractions? Are the pupils using the correct vocabulary: whole, equal parts, equivalent, same, four equal parts, one half, two halves, a quarter, two quarters, three quarters?

Extension: Draw a square with half shaded and the other half blank in quarters. **Ask:** *Does the unshaded part of the square show a half? Explain your reasoning.*

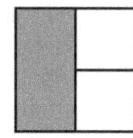

Support: Provide pupils with fraction shapes so they can see which fractions are identical or linked.

Coin swap

Strand: Measurement

Learning objective: To find different combinations of coins that equal the same amounts of money.

You will need: A large amount of real money (1ps, 2ps, 5ps, 10ps, 20ps, 50ps and £s)

1. **Say:** *Today we will be learning more about money and how we can use different coins to create equivalent values.*

2. Draw a pound symbol (£) on the board. **Ask:** *What does this symbol mean? Where have you seen it?* **Say:** *This symbol represents the pound and we see it when we buy things.*

3. **Ask:** *What other symbols do we see when we go shopping?*

4. Discuss the pence symbol (p) and that one pound has a larger value/is worth more than one pence. **Ask:** *How many pence are there in a pound?* **Say:** *There are 100 pence in a pound.*

5. Show a 50p. **Ask:** *What coin is this? How do you know? Are there any clues to tell us that it is a 50p coin?* (inscription)

6. **Ask:** *Is there any other way we can make 50p? Can you show me? Is there another way? How many ways are there to make 50p with the coins we have here?* Encourage the pupils to make 50p using a systematic approach, starting with combinations of the largest value coins.

7. Repeat this with £1, 20p and 10p, each time asking how many different ways there are to make the amount.

Key checks: Can the pupils recognise the coins without reading the amount on the coin? Are the pupils using the correct vocabulary: money, coin, pence, pound, equivalent, value, worth?

Extension: Put an item for sale on the table, e.g. a toy for 68p, and ask the pupils to find as many different ways of making the amount as possible. **Ask:** *What is the largest number of coins you can use?* (68 pennies) *What is the smallest number of coins you can use?* (5 coins: 50p, 10p, 5p, 2p and 1p)

Support: Focus on how many 1ps are equivalent to certain coins. Look at 2p, 5p and 10p first. Can pupils use their money to create number bonds to 10? Use 1ps first and then extend to large representations, e.g. 2p + 2p = 4p, 5p + 1p = 6p, 6p + 4p = 10p.

Shortest to longest

Strand: Measurement

Learning objective: To be able to compare and order lengths and record the results using >, < and =.

You will need: whiteboards, whiteboard pens, board rubbers, a measuring tape, rulers, a variety of objects of different lengths (e.g. books, toys, pencils, glue sticks)

1. **Ask:** *Who is the tallest person here?* Give each pupil a whiteboard and ask them to line up from tallest to shortest, holding their whiteboards.

2. Measure each pupil and write their heights on their whiteboards.

3. Write the symbols < > and = on individual whiteboards for the pupils to see.

4. **Ask:** *Can you use the inequalities symbols (<, =, >) to say who is taller out of (name four pupils)?* Answers might look like: pupil 1 < pupil 2 < pupil 3 < pupil 4.

5. Mix up the pupils so that they are in a different order.

6. **Ask:** *Can you use the symbols again to make this number sentence make sense?* (could change to, e.g. pupil 4 > pupil 1 > pupil 3 > pupil 2).

7. Show the pupils a variety of objects. Ask them to measure the objects to the nearest cm and put them in order from longest to shortest.

8. Once this has been completed, ask them to write the objects as a number sentence, e.g. rubber < glue stick < pencil < work book < text book; 3cm < 6cm < 7cm < 15cm <20cm.

9. Ask the pupils to rearrange the objects and make another number sentence.

10. Repeat this activity with other objects.

Key checks: Can each pupil hold a ruler correctly? Do the pupils know where to measure from? Are the pupils using the correct vocabulary: length, width, height, depth, long, longer, longest, short, shorter, shortest, tall, taller, tallest, high, higher, highest?

Extension: Pupils compare objects that are very close in size.

Support: Allow pupils to begin comparing using 'bigger than, smaller than, larger than, equal, same'. Only compare two objects/people at a time.

Mass order

Strand: Measurement

Learning objective: To estimate, compare and order mass and record the results using >, < and =.

You will need: whiteboards, whiteboard pens, board rubbers, a variety of different objects, each with a different mass (e.g. toys, books, glue sticks, pencils), balance scales

1. Show the pupils the objects and **ask:** *Which object do you think is the heaviest? Why?*

2. **Ask:** *What is estimating?* Remind pupils that it is sensible guessing, using what they know.

3. **Say:** *We are going to estimate which is the lightest and which is the heaviest object here.*

4. Ask the pupils to lift up each of the objects and to write them down in the order they think they should go, using the symbols < and > to make a number sentence, e.g. pencil < glue stick < toy < book.

5. As a group, weigh the objects using the balance scales.

6. Ask the pupils to write down the correct order to see if their estimates were correct.

7. Repeat this activity with other objects.

Key checks: Can the pupils remember the name for each symbol: is more than and is less than? Are the pupils using the correct vocabulary: weigh, weighs, balances, heavy, heavier, heaviest, light, lighter, lightest, mass?

Extension: Pupils compare objects that look close in weight; this will support their future ideas.

Support: Allow the pupils to begin comparing using the language 'more than, less than, larger, equal, same'. Only compare two objects at a time.

Capacity crew

Strand: Measurement

Learning objective: To be able to estimate, compare and order capacity and record the results using >, < and =.

You will need: a variety of containers (different sizes) labelled A, B, C, etc., small containers (e.g. small yoghurt pots), a source of water, whiteboards, whiteboard pens, board rubbers, a measuring jug that features a scale

1. Show the pupils the variety of containers and **ask:** *Which container do you think holds the most water? Why?*

2. **Ask:** *What is estimating?* Remind pupils that it is sensible guessing, using what they know.

3. **Say:** *We are going to estimate which container holds the most water.*

4. Ask the pupils to use the symbols < and > to make a number sentence, e.g. container B < container C < container A < container D.

5. As a group, measure how much water each container holds, using the yoghurt pots.

6. Ask the pupils to write down the correct order to see if their estimates were correct.

7. Measure how much each container holds in mL by pouring the water into a measuring jug. Discuss that we measure capacity in millilitres and litres.

8. Repeat this activity with more containers.

Key checks: Can the pupils remember what 'estimate' means? Can the pupils read the scale on a measuring jug? Are the pupils using the correct vocabulary: container, volume, capacity, most, least, more than, less than, millilitres, litres, scale?

Extension: Allow the pupils to measure accurately in mL up to 100mL.

Support: Allow the pupils to begin comparing using the language 'more than, less than, larger, equal, same'. Only compare two containers at a time.

Time o'clock

Strand: Measurement

Learning objectives: To tell and write the time to five minutes, including quarter past/to the hour and draw the hands on a clock face to show these times. Know the number of minutes in an hour and the number of hours in a day.

You will need: analogue clocks, printed sheet of analogue clocks (for pupils to draw hands on), paper plate, rulers, pencils

1. **Say:** *Today we will be learning about how to tell the time using a clock.*

2. **Ask:** *What do we already know about time?* Take pupils' answers.

3. **Say:** *A clock has small increments/marks that indicate one minute and there are 60 minutes in an hour* (point to individual minutes and the five-minute increments).

4. **Ask:** *Can anyone show me one o'clock on their clock?*

5. Show one o'clock on your clock and point out where the big and small hands point.

6. Repeat for different o'clock times and then move onto half past times.

7. Show the pupils a paper plate and fold it in half. **Say:** *This represents half past.* Fold the plate in half again and **say:** *This is quarter past.* Unfold the plate to show the quarter marks. Point out quarter past and quarter to.

8. Show the pupils your analogue clock with the time 10:15 and explain that this time reads quarter past 10.

9. **Say:** *When the big hand is on 3, it is quarter past.* Repeat with quarter to when the big hand is on 9.

10. Repeat with the five-minute increments and count around the clock in fives whilst pointing at the correct place (5, 10, 15, etc.).

11. Distribute the printed analogue clocks and say certain times, e.g. quarter past five, and ask the pupils to draw in the correct hands.

Key checks: Do the pupils understand the increase in time when they count the five-minute increments? Do the pupils understand the terms 'past' and 'to'? Are the pupils using the key vocabulary: o'clock, past, to, minute, hour, time, quarter past, quarter to, clock, long hand, short hand?

Extension: Show the pupils six clock faces with different times on them. **Ask:** *Which clock faces show a time between four and six o'clock? Can you explain your thinking? Can you create a time between four and six o'clock?*

Support: Pupils to focus on consolidation of o'clock and half past.

2-D bingo

Strand: Geometry – properties of shapes

Learning objective: To name and describe 2-D shapes.

You will need: 2-D shapes (e.g. squares, triangles, rectangles, circles, pentagons, hexagons, octagons) and a variety of quadrilaterals (e.g. rhombus, trapezium, kite), whiteboards, whiteboard pens, board rubbers

1. **Ask:** *What 2-D shapes do we know the names of?* Give pupils time to answer and add to their suggestions if needed. Write the list on the whiteboard.

2. As a group, write and draw each shape on the whiteboard so pupils can see the visual and written representation.

3. Ask the pupils to make bingo boards by splitting their whiteboards into six sections and drawing a shape in each section.

4. **Say:** *You are going to play 2-D shape bingo. I will describe a shape and if you have that shape on your board you cross it off. The winner is the first player who has crossed off all six of their shapes. You will need to shout 'Bingo' when you cross off your final shape.*

Key checks: Do the pupils understand the properties of each shape as you describe them (which part is the side, vertices or face, etc.)? Use descriptions such as: • **Square:** I have four sides, all the same length, and four vertices. • **Hexagon:** I have six straight sides and six vertices. • **Triangle:** I have three straight sides and three vertices. • **Circle:** I have one curved side and zero vertices. • **Rectangle:** I have four sides, two are short and two are long. I have four vertices. • **Pentagon:** I have five straight sides and five vertices. • **Rhombus:** I have four straight sides, all of equal length. My opposite sides are parallel and my opposite angles are equal. Are the pupils using the correct vocabulary: flat, curved, straight, round, circle, triangle, square, rectangle, long, short, 2-D, squares, triangles, rectangles, circles, pentagons, hexagons, octagons, quadrilaterals, rhombus, trapezium, kite?

Extension: Pupils become the bingo caller and describe the shapes for others.

Support: Pupils focus on core shapes (square, rectangle, triangle, circle).

Shapes wanted

Strand: Geometry – properties of shapes

Learning objective: To name and describe 3-D shapes.

You will need: a whiteboard, whiteboard pen, board rubber, 3-D shapes (spheres, cubes, cuboids, prisms (a variety of), pyramids and cones)

1. **Ask:** *What 3-D shapes do we know the names of?*

2. Allow pupils to answer and add to their suggestions if needed.

3. Write these names on the whiteboard and link them with the physical shapes you have so that the pupils can see the visual and written representation.

4. **Say:** *There is a shape here that is wanted, she has broken the law in shape town!*

5. Explain that as a group you will create a wanted poster so that this shape may be caught.

6. As a group, write a wanted poster for a cube on the whiteboard. Hold the cube and count the number of edges, faces and vertices (corners). Ask the pupils to tell you the properties of the shape and add them to the poster, e.g. WANTED! This mean, despicable shape has 6 disgusting faces, 12 hideous edges, but be careful as she also has 8 sharp vertices!

7. Once you have completed a group poster, allow the pupils to create their own posters to describe the shapes. (Write the descriptive words/phrases and ask the pupils to add the number properties of the shapes.)

8. Pupils share their posters and you check their understanding of the task.

Key checks: Can the pupils name the shapes on sight? Are the pupils using the correct vocabulary: flat, curved, straight, round, faces, sides, edges, vertices, rectangular, long, short, spheres, cubes, cuboids, prisms, cones?

Extension: Pupils describe more challenging shapes: hexagonal prisms and square-based pyramids.

Support: Pupils focus on cubes and cuboids and one other prism.

Shape sorting

Strand: Geometry – properties of shapes

Learning objective: To sort and classify shapes.

You will need: 2-D shapes (squares, triangles, rectangles, circles, pentagons, hexagons, octagons, rhombus), 3-D shapes (spheres, cubes, cuboids, prisms (a variety of), pyramids and cones), whiteboards, whiteboard pens, board rubbers

1. Show the pupils a variety of mixed-size 2-D and 3-D shapes.

2. **Ask:** *Can you sort the shapes in front of you into 2-D and 3-D piles?*

3. Ask pupils to split their whiteboard into two sections and label one section 2-D and the other 3-D.

4. **Ask:** *Can you write down the names of the shapes that are 2-D and the names of the shapes that are 3-D in the correct places on your whiteboard?*

5. Draw a Carroll diagram on your whiteboard like this:

	Square faces	Not Square faces
2-D shapes		
3-D shapes		

6. You may need to explain to the pupils how a Carroll diagram works.

7. Once the pupils have sorted the shapes, they could change the headings of the Carroll diagram and sort the shapes differently.

Key checks: Make sure the pupils are using each 2-D and 3-D shape so that they are independently checking their thinking. Are the pupils using the correct vocabulary: flat, curved, straight, round, circle, triangle, square, rectangle, long, short, faces, sides, edges, vertices, long, short, spheres, cubes, cuboids, prisms, cones?

Extension: Pupils come up with their own headings for the Carroll diagram.

Support: Pupils focus on 2-D shapes only, followed by 3-D shapes only.

Shapes within shapes

Strand: Geometry – properties of shapes

Learning objective: To identify 2-D shapes on the surface of 3-D shapes.

You will need: 2-D shapes (squares, triangles, rectangles, circles, pentagons, hexagons, octagons, rhombus), 3-D shapes (spheres, cubes, cuboids, prisms (a variety of), pyramids and cones), whiteboards, whiteboard pens, board rubbers

1. Show the pupils a cube and **ask:** *What can you tell me about this shape?* Pupils may suggest the name of the shape or some of its properties.

2. **Say:** *The faces of this cube are a 2-D shape.*

3. **Ask:** *Can you name the shape?* (square)

4. **Say:** *A cube has six square faces.* Allow the pupils to see this and feel this too.

5. Show the pupils a cuboid and repeat the above process.

6. As a group, **say:** *This cuboid has two square (or differently sized rectangular) faces and four rectangular faces (differently sized rectangles).*

7. Tell the pupils that they are going to create a poster that shows the 2-D shapes that make the faces of the 3-D shapes. Pupils should have access to 2-D shapes that they can trace around if wanted/needed.

8. Allow the pupils to share their work and comment about the 2-D shapes that they can see.

Key checks: Are the pupils using the correct vocabulary: flat, curved, straight, round, circle, triangle, square, rectangle, long, short, faces, sides, edges, vertices, rectangle, long, short, spheres, cubes, cuboids, prisms, cones?

Extension: Explore the 2-D shape types that make up the faces of 3-D shapes. Record your findings. Do any 3-D shapes have only one face type? Two different 2-D shape face types? Do any shapes have less than two 2-D shape faces? Investigate the number of vertices and number of faces. What do you notice?

Support: Provide pupils with 2-D and 3-D shapes. Get pupils to stick the 2-D shape on to the 3-D shape. Write on the face with a whiteboard pen.

Symmetrical bugs

Strand: Geometry – properties of shapes

Learning objective: To identify symmetry in 2-D shapes.

You will need: whiteboards, whiteboard pens, board rubbers

1. **Say:** *Today we are looking at special ladybirds that have a line of symmetry.*

2. **Ask:** *Does anyone know what symmetry is?*

3. **Say:** *Symmetry is having one side that is the mirror image of another.*

4. Draw a circle/oval (ladybird), put a line down the middle and draw three dots on one side only. Ask the pupils to copy the picture.

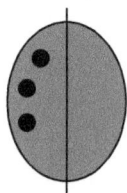

5. **Ask:** *If symmetry is having one side an exact reflection of the other, what should the other side look like? Can you draw it?* Let pupils draw the dots on their ladybirds.

6. Show the pupils the symmetry and ask them to check their work.

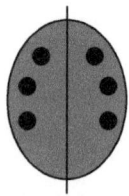

7. Ask the pupils to draw their own symmetrical ladybirds and check for understanding of key language.

Key checks: Ensure pupils know where the line of symmetry should go. Are the pupils using the correct vocabulary: symmetrical, line of symmetry, fold, match, mirror line, reflection, pattern, repeating pattern?

Extension: Pupils could use different shapes to reflect. Pupils go outside and investigate symmetry in the playground/school.

Support: Allow pupils to use smaller numbers to begin building confidence.

Robot right angle turns

Strand: Geometry – position and direction

Learning objective: To recognise right angles and quarter turns.

You will need: whiteboards, whiteboard pens, board rubbers, objects/small toys, circles with quarter marks

1. **Say:** *Today we will be investigating right angle turns.*

2. **Ask:** *Does anyone know what a right angle is?*

3. **Say:** *A right angle is equal to a one quarter turn.*

4. Show a quarter turn using a circle, starting at A and turning to B:

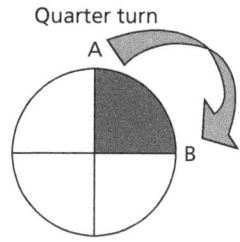

Quarter turn

5. **Ask:** *How many quarter turns are in a half turn?* (2) Show the pupils this by turning one quarter then another one quarter.

6. Give the pupils an object/small toy and instruct them to turn it 1, 2, 3 or 4 quarters so that you can check their understanding.

Key checks: Do pupils know how many quarter turns there are in a full rotation? Are the pupils using the correct vocabulary: right angle, quarter turn, rotation, clockwise, anticlockwise, straight line, 90 degree turn?

Extension: Adult to position toys facing in different directions. Can the pupils describe how many quarter turns it would take each toy to face the front of the room?

Support: Provide pupils with a circle that is split into four quarters so that they can see the quarter turns.

Robot pupils

Strand: Geometry – position and direction

Learning objective: To describe and direct positions.

You will need: a 10 × 10 grid (A–J, 1–10) made of tape on the floor or drawn in chalk in the playground, small grids (A–D, 1–5)

1. **Say:** *Today I am going to be controlling you for a little while! You will be following my instructions to move around a grid.*

2. Take the pupils to the grid and **ask:** *What do you see?*

3. **Say:** *Going across the grid at the bottom we have the letters A to J. Going up the grid, you can see the numbers 1 to 10. We read the grid by saying the letter first and then the number.*

4. **Ask:** *Can someone go and stand in A2?* Ask one pupil to stand in A2.

5. **Say:** *It might help you to remember how to read the grid to think about walking along the corridor (across – letters) and then going up the stairs (go up – numbers).*

6. Instruct the pupil to move around the grid, e.g. *Take one step forward, turn right and walk two steps forward.* Each time you instruct the pupil, ask the others *Which grid location is he/she on now?* (B3, etc.)

7. Encourage the pupils to take turns guiding each other around the grid and then write the coordinates of each location they stop at.

Key checks: Are the pupils writing the coordinates correctly (A,1), using 'along the corridor and up the stairs'? Are the pupils using the correct vocabulary: position, over, under, underneath, above, below, top, bottom, side, on, in, outside, inside, around, in front, behind, front, back?

Extension: Pupils draw their own grid (or use a print-out) and create a route to travel whilst recording each move (A,1) to (B,2).

Support: Provide a smaller grid A–D and 1–5.

Simple statistics

Strand: Statistics

Learning objective: To interpret and construct simple pictograms.

You will need: whiteboards, whiteboard pens, board rubbers

1. **Ask:** *Does anyone know how we collect information?*

2. **Say:** *In maths, another word for information is data. Data is often collected by asking a question. Today we are going to ask some questions to help us collect data and then represent it using images. We call this a pictogram – because we use pictures to show data.*

3. **Say:** *We are going to begin by investigating the eye colour of everyone here.*

4. Draw a table on the board and ask the pupils what colour their eyes are. Invite each pupil to come up to the board and add tally marks to the chart to represent their eye colour. Help them if needed. For example:

Eye colour	Tally	Number
Blue	ЖŤ I	6
Green	I I	2
Brown	I I I I	4

5. Discuss why we use tally marks to collect data.

6. Draw a pictogram to represent the information collected in the tally chart. For example:

Eye colour	
Blue	👁 👁 👁 👁 👁 👁
Green	👁 👁
Brown	👁 👁 👁 👁

Continues

7. Ask pupils to use the tally chart and pictogram to answer questions about the information. (e.g. Which eye colour is the most common? Which eye colour is the least common?)

8. **Ask:** *Can you create a table and pictogram that shows hair colour?*

9. Assist pupils to create a tally chart and to select a suitable image to use. Ask them to double check that the information in the tally chart and pictogram matches.

Key checks: Can pupils tally correctly? (Cross through on five) Can they create pictograms from the data collected? Can they use the tally chart and pictogram to answer questions about the data, e.g. *Which colour is the most/least common? How many people have the same colour eyes/hair as you? Can you tell me something about this pictogram?* Are the pupils using the key vocabulary: count, tally, sort, pictogram, represent, group, set, list, table, label, title, most popular, most common, least popular, least common?

Extension: Pupils investigate their own questions.

Support: Practise tallying different numbers so that pupils explore tallying five and above. Pupils focus on drawing the pictogram rather than the table and pictogram.

IMPACT
Intervention
English Activities

Snappy sorting

Strand: Reading – word reading

Learning objective: To accurately read words by blending known sounds.

You will need: whiteboard, whiteboard pen, board rubber, set of pre-prepared words tailored to support the pupils you are working with (e.g. words containing ee/ea/e_e or ou/ow)

1. **Say:** *Let's review one of the sounds you know. I'd like you to write all the different ways you know of writing that sound.* (Tell pupils which sound.) Write all the different ways of writing the sound on a whiteboard.

2. **Say:** *Here are some words that contain the sound ee/ea/e_e.* Spread the words out on the table. **Ask:** *Can you sort the words into groups containing the same way of writing ee/ea/e_e?*

3. **Say:** *Now you have organised the words into a list, I'd like you to say each sound in the word on its own, then blend the whole word together. Like this: th-r-ee, three.* Slowly bring your hands together as you blend the word, ending with a clap as you say 'three'.

4. Repeat with each word from the list.

Key checks: Are the pupils using pure sounds and not saying the schwa sound when they are sounding out? For example, 'd-r-ea-m' easily blends to 'dream'. 'Duh-ruh-ea-muh' blends to 'dareamer'. Better readers often miss the sounding out step, but insist every pupil does this. It is common that pupils make mistakes and mis-read words, e.g. 'place' and 'palace'.

Extension: Offer pupils longer words that contain more than one syllable. Words should also contain more than one digraph (underlined), e.g. Ch<u>i</u>n<u>e</u>se, dr<u>ea</u>m<u>er</u>, b<u>ee</u>k<u>ee</u>per.

Support: Focus on one sound at a time. Before asking the pupil to sound out and blend the word, **say:** *Where is the sound 'ee'?* Continue to sound out and blend the word. Mix up the order of the words and repeat. Encourage the pupil to sound out and blend as quickly as possible. Model and have the pupil copy.

My word family

Strand: Reading – word reading

Learning objective: To identify and read suffixes and the root word.

You will need: a selection of words (see step 3) prepared on card

1. **Say:** *Let's look at some words.* **Ask:** *Can you clap the syllables?* For example, helpful has two claps: help-ful.

2. **Ask:** *Can you fold the card so the suffix is on one side of the fold and the root word on the other?*

3. **Ask:** *Can you sort the cards into word families?* Once word families have been established, examine each word in turn and look at how the suffix alters the meaning of the word. The first column contains the root word.

Help	helpful	helpless			
Hope	hopeful	hopeless			
Tight			tightly		tightness
State			stately	statement	
Taste	tasteful	tasteless			
Entertain				entertainment	
Dark			darkly		darkness

4. **Say:** *I'm going to arrange the word cards on the table to form a grid.* Start placing the word cards on the table to match the layout shown above.

5. **Ask:** *Can you work out how I am arranging the words?* As you work through each word family, encourage the pupils to look at the layout of the cards on the table and to add words in the correct place, giving reasons for doing so.

6. **Say:** *You have noticed I am organising the words by the suffix.* **Ask:** *Can you explain how each suffix alters the meaning of the word?* **Say:** *Adding the suffix -ful to a word changes the meaning of the word to 'lots of' or 'full of' something. -less changes the meaning of the word to 'without' something. When the suffix -ly is added, the root word becomes an adverb. -ment and -ness change the root word into a noun.*

Continues

7. In groups of between three and six pupils, play 'Suffix families' with the cards (not including root words or 'entertainment'). Shuffle the word cards and deal the same number to each player. The object of the game is to collect all the words in one suffix family. Each player looks at their cards and hides them from the other players. All players place a card they do not want face down on the table and say *Pass it on* together. Each player slides the card to the player on their left. Players pick up the new word and see if they want to keep it, or continue to pass it on. Players continue to pass cards, until someone has collected all the cards in one suffix family. They say *I have a suffix family!*

Key checks: Can pupils identify a group of letters that form a suffix?

Extension: During the game, pupils ask the player on their right to give them a card containing a certain suffix, e.g. **say:** *Can I have a card with the suffix -ly?* If the pupil has a card, they must pass it on. If they do not, they **say:** *I don't have it.*

Support: Concentrate on two suffixes during the session. Revisit the session to introduce further suffixes.

Lousy letters

Strand: Reading – word reading

Learning objective: To fluently read common exception words.

You will need: a set of 10 exception words taken from the list in Appendix 1 of the national curriculum, or from your school's phonics programme

Here are a selection of words from Appendix 1: door, floor, poor, because, find, kind, mind, behind, pupil, pupils, wild, climb, most, only, both, old, cold, gold, hold, told, every, everybody, even, great, break, steak, pretty, beautiful, after, fast, last, past, father, class, grass, pass, plant, path, bath, hour, move, prove, improve, sure, sugar, eye, could, should, would, who, whole, any, many, clothes, busy, people, water, again, half, money, Mr, Mrs, parents, Christmas.

1. **Say:** *We are going to learn to read these tricky words without blending them. Each one contains lousy letters that do not follow our rules.*

2. **Ask:** *What are the lousy letters in this word?* Show the pupils a word, e.g. 'kind'. **Say:** *The lousy letter is 'i' because we would expect it to be a short 'i' sound, but it isn't.* **Say:** *kind,* without sounding out and blending. **Say:** *Repeat the word.*

3. Repeat step 2 with the other words.

4. **Say:** *I'm going to show you three of the words. How quickly can you read the word?* Turn all the words face down and pick up three. Hide these in your hand and flash them at the pupils in a random order. Repeat each word a few times, getting faster.

5. **Ask:** *Does anyone want to be the teacher and flash the words?* Select a pupil, who will choose three different words.

Key checks: Can pupils identify the letter or letters that are the lousy letters?

Extension: Work with more words in each session.

Support: Work with fewer words. Make sure you still flash the words quickly so pupils are reading without blending.

Which is which?

Strand: Reading – word reading

Learning objective: To quickly and accurately read common words.

You will need: a range of related or commonly confused words made into flashcards (e.g. some/same, make/made, polite/police, through/though), the following prepared sentences (on paper or the whiteboard) without the underlined words included:

Yesterday, I <u>made</u> a delicious cake.

Make sure you are always <u>polite</u>.

I would like to have <u>some</u> yogurt for my pudding today.

Did you see he went <u>through</u> the tunnel?

1. **Say:** *There is a fine balance between reading fluently, which means quickly and carefully, and just reading quickly. Sometimes, good readers make mistakes by not checking carefully. Today we will focus on checking carefully.*

2. Show the pupils the flashcards. **Ask:** *Can you make pairs with the similar words?*

3. **Say:** *These sentences only make sense with one of the words from the pair.* **Ask:** *Can you decide if it is the correct word or not?* For example, show pupils the sentence 'Yesterday, I _____ a delicious cake' with the flashcard 'make' in the space. Repeat for all the words.

4. Make sentences using either the correct or incorrect word. Pupils need to read the sentence and give a thumbs up or thumbs down depending on whether the sentence makes sense or not. **Say:** *Hide your thumb behind your back. Read the sentence in your head. Now, 1, 2, 3, show me, thumbs up or thumbs down?* Remind pupils to be fluent not just fast readers.

Key checks: Are the pupils able to notice the similarities and differences between the words? Are the pupils able to read accurately?

Extension: Create sentences using the word that was not used. Pupils could either alter the existing sentence so it fits the word, or create a new sentence, e.g. I make a delicious cake.

Support: Ask the pupils to read these and other similar words. These will need to be prepared on flashcards, e.g. come/came, see/seen, prince/princess, where/were. Once the pupils are confident enough to read these on flashcards, you could write a list of 10 words on a whiteboard and see how quickly they can read all the words accurately.

Guided group reading

Strand: Reading – word reading

Learning objective: To read fluently and with confidence, decoding words accurately.

You will need: post-it notes, a piece of text that is at the correct level for the pupil

The text should be at a level where the pupil may need to sound out one in every 10 words, or fewer. If a pupil is having to sound out more words than this, they will not be able to understand the text well.

It is possible you will do guided group reading, where small groups of pupils read the same text at the same time.

1. **Ask:** *What is the title of the book? What do you think the book is about? Can you say what the story may be about?* **Say:** *Look at the information on the front and back cover, as well as the illustrations.*

2. **Say:** *Skim and scan through the book and find the characters' names. Now close the book.*

3. **Say:** *Now let's read the story. As we read, look for words to describe the setting.* **Ask:** *Can you write the words or phrases on post-it notes?*

4. **Say:** *There are some words in this book that have lousy letters. I found the words 'half' and 'everybody'. Can you find any more?*

5. **Say:** *If you can't read a word you should sound it out and blend it back together, then re-read the sentence.*

6. **Say:** *Let's read the book again.* **Ask:** *Can you add lots of expression?* **Say:** *You should try to use a 'story-time' voice and read with lots of expression to make the book sound as interesting as you can.*

Key checks: Is the text at the correct level for this pupil? Fluency check – do one in every 10 words need to be sounded out?

Extension: Trickier books often have more punctuation. Ensure pupils are responding appropriately to punctuation and using a 'story-time' voice – pausing at commas, longer pause at full stops, changing their voice to respond to speech marks, question marks and exclamation marks.

Support: Ensure pupils are able to read all the words before starting to read. You may need to spend time with the words on flashcards, reading the words quickly as with the 'lousy letters' activity.

The next link

Strand: Reading – comprehension

Learning objective: To be able to put events in order in a story or say how information is linked.

You will need: 5–6 pictures from a familiar story to sequence, non-fiction books around the same theme (e.g. festivals and celebrations), whiteboard, whiteboard pen, board rubber

Fiction

1. **Ask:** *Can you tell me what the story is about from your memory?* If pupils are not confident, read the story.

2. **Say:** *Here are some pictures from the story. Can you put the pictures in the correct order to match the story?* Ensure all pupils are participating.

3. **Say:** *Now let's use the book to check that the pictures are in the correct order.*

Non-fiction

1. **Say:** *These books were all in the same topic box, but I can't work out why they should be together. This one is about Eid, this one is about Harvest festival.* **Ask:** *Can you work out what the link is?*

2. **Say:** *Look through the books to find links.* For example, find special food in one book and look through others to see if they contain information about special food too. **Say:** *Does each book contain information about special clothes? Music? Gifts?*

3. **Say:** *The books are linked by the topic.* Write a list on the whiteboard to be clear that although the books do not have the same title, they are related because they are all about festivals and celebrations.

Key checks: Can the pupils re-tell the story from memory? Can the pupils find information that is linked?

Extension: Select a story that pupils are less familiar with.

Support: Give just three pictures to the pupils to sequence. Add a fourth picture and **ask:** *Where would this picture go?* Have a checklist prepared, so the pupils know what they are looking for with non-fiction books.

Our favourite traditional tale

Strand: Reading – comprehension

Learning objective: To be able to confidently tell a range of fairy and traditional tales.

You will need: a basket containing a range of storyteller props (e.g. a pair of grandma's glasses and shawl, Red Riding Hood's cloak and basket, wolf ears on a headband, a magic wand, a special 'storyteller' hat), a number of traditional and fairy tales including *Hansel and Gretel, Snow White, Little Red Riding Hood, The Three Little Pigs, Jack and the Beanstalk, Cinderella, The Elves and the Shoemaker*

1. **Say:** *It's storytime. In the basket are some of our favourite traditional tales.* Carefully select a prop so that you become part of the story. **Say:** *I am going to choose this hat to wear while I retell the story, because it will help me concentrate.* Stand up and tell the story in an engaging way, moving around the space, making eye contact with pupils and varying your voice.

2. (Could be a second session) **Say:** *Today it's your turn to become the story teller. Select a prop from the basket. You will need to include what happens in the story and what the characters say as you retell the story.* **Ask:** *How will you make the story as exciting to listen to as possible?* Allow pupils time to prepare what they will say.

3. Pupils retell their version of the story. During this time, act like a member of the group, modelling respectful listening.

4. **Ask:** *What did you enjoy?* Encourage pupils to make positive comments about each other's retelling.

Key checks: Does the pupil know the story well? They shouldn't need to refer to the book. Does the pupil vary their voice and engage the listener? Some pupils will not feel confident enough to speak in front of a large group, so select a smaller group for them to re-tell the story to.

Extension: Select a less well-known story for the pupil to re-tell, e.g. a Hans Christian Anderson fairy tale such as *The Tinderbox Soldier* or *The Twelve Swans*.

Support: Support pupils during the preparation phase by practising telling the story without an audience. **Ask:** *What comes next?* if a pupil gets 'stuck'.

Can my question be answered?

Strand: Reading – comprehension

Learning objective: To ask questions and use a variety of non-fiction books to find the answers.

You will need: non-fiction books, ideally these should be linked to the same topic, post-it notes, pencils

1. Show the books. Look carefully at the titles but do not look inside.

2. **Ask:** *Which book would you most like to read? What would you like to find out?*

3. Support pupils to ask a variety of questions using different question words: 'what', 'who', 'where', 'when', 'why', 'are there', 'can' and 'do'. Ensure pupils speak in full sentences. They should write their questions on post-it notes.

4. Look at one of the questions, e.g. 'Are there more than 300 types of duck?' Model the thought process for finding the answer to this question. **Say:** *I am looking for a book with information about birds. This book about world animals may have the answer. I can scan the contents page for the word 'birds' or 'ducks'. It's not there. I can use the index. Here is 'd' for 'ducks'. Turn to page __. I'm now going to scan the sub-headings. Here we are!* If none of the books answer the question, look at the book you think is the best match, but say you will need further information.

5. In pairs, ask the pupils to select a question and decide which book to look at. If they find the answer, they should write it on the original question post-it note.

6. Review the questions and answers at the end of the session. **Say:** *Which features of non-fiction books made it easier to find the information?* (e.g. the contents page, index page, glossary, headings, sub-headings, labels or fact boxes) Point these features out in a book as each one is named. Label a post-it note for each and stick it in the correct position on the page.

Key checks: Can the pupils ask a question, using a question word? Do they make considered choices about which book to use to answer the question? Do they use the features of the book to help them find the answer or do they flick through the book? Do pupils understand the key vocabulary: contents page, index page, glossary, headings, sub-headings, labels, fact boxes?

Extension: Have questions prepared that may require the pupil to look at and interpret information from a diagram or graph.

Support: Have questions prepared and a book at an easier level that will allow the pupil to access the information.

Join in!

Strand: Reading – comprehension

Learning objective: To recognise recurring language in stories and poetry.

You will need: stories written in rhyme or traditional tales with repeated phrases (e.g. *The Gingerbread Man*)

1. **Say:** *We are looking for parts of the story that are repeated. I want you to work out when they are coming up and to join in and say them.*

2. Start to read one of the stories, emphasising the rhyme and pattern of the language. Have the book positioned so the pupils are able to see it easily.

3. After the phrase has been repeated a few times, **ask:** *How do you know when the repeated phrase is going to happen?* Allow time for the pupils to think and take feedback. Pupils should offer that there are one or two words before the repeated part. **Say:** *Well done, you have noticed the clue.*

4. **Ask:** *Do you know any other stories that have repeated phrases?* Allow pupils time to think and take feedback. Traditional tales often have repeating phrases, for example the giant in *Jack and the Beanstalk* says 'Fee, fi, fo, fum.' The wolf in *The Three Little Pigs* says 'I'll huff and I'll puff and I'll blow your house down.'

5. In another session, read a different rhyming story or poem with a repeated phrase.

_____

Key checks: Can pupils recognise a repeated refrain and join in?

Extension: Point out other repeated structures within the story. Some stories have a longer repeated section than others.

Support: Pupils may need support to recognise the repeated refrain. Read the story more than once, on different occasions, to allow pupils to join in.

Lovely language

Strand: Reading – comprehension

Learning objectives: To learn new words and discuss favourite words and phrases. To answer questions about what has been read to show understanding.

You will need: a story book containing words pupils may not be familiar with, a whiteboard, whiteboard pen, board rubber

1. **Say:** *I'm going to read a story. Every time I say a word and you don't know what it means, I want you to shoot your hand out in a stop motion.*

2. **Ask:** *Which word is new?* Praise pupils for stopping to clarify the meaning of a word. **Say:** *I'm really pleased you asked because that is a tricky word.*

3. **Say:** *These are the new words you spotted.* Write them on a whiteboard.

4. Having discussed the meaning of the new words, re-read the story without interruption. This could be at a different time.

5. **Ask:** *Can you use some of the new words in your own sentences?*

6. **Say:** *I like this phrase* (find an alliterative phrase) *because it is alliterative – both words start with the same letter and they give a good picture in your mind about that part of the story.* **Ask:** *Which phrase do you particularly like? Why?*

Key checks: Can the pupils recognise that they do not know a particular word? Some pupils are so busy decoding, they lack understanding of familiar and new words. Can the pupils quickly understand the meaning of new words?

Extension: Ask the pupils to write a list of words they are unsure of from their own reading.

Support: Offer pupils phrases from the story to discuss. **Ask:** *Which of these phrases do you really like? Can you say what you like about it?*

Perfect poetry

Strand: Reading – comprehension

Learning objective: To recite poetry from memory.

You will need: a book of pupils' poetry (choose poems of no more than eight lines)

1. **Say:** *We are going to learn some poetry.* **Ask:** *What does recite mean?* **Say:** *'Recite' means to remember and say or sing out loud.*

2. Read the poem.

3. **Say:** *I'd like you to repeat each line after me.* Once pupils are confidently repeating each line, link the first two lines together. They should then repeat two lines together until confident. (So, lines 3 and 4, lines 5 and 6 and lines 7 and 8.) Gradually build up larger chunks, until the pupils can remember the whole poem.

4. Look at the type of voice needed to turn the recital into a performance. **Say:** *How can we vary our voices as we read the poem?*

5. **Ask:** *Who is confident to recite the poem?* You could **say:** *I like the way you changed your voice to a whisper there, because it's quiet in the poem!*

6. **Say:** *We are going to add some actions or pauses to our recital of the poem.*

7. Repeat for other poems. **Say:** *Can you prepare and recite a different poem from this book?*

Key checks: Can the pupils remember and recite the poem on a different day?

Extension: Select a slightly longer poem to learn and recite, or a poem containing humour, which requires dramatic pauses.

Support: Select a slightly shorter poem to learn and recite.

That doesn't sound right!

Strand: Reading – comprehension

Learning objective: To check the text makes sense when read aloud and correct any inaccuracies.

You will need: a set of stories that are the same (e.g. guided group reading books), puppet (optional)

1. **Say:** *We are going to play a game. The puppet is going to read the book and may make some mistakes. I want you to follow along in your book and if he makes a mistake, you say 'That doesn't sound right!'* The pupils should then correct the word and re-read the whole sentence.

2. Misread one word every one or two sentences, focusing on words you know the group finds particularly tricky, e.g. if the group confuses *me* and *my*, focus on these words.

3. **Say:** *Well done, you stopped the puppet and corrected the misread word.* Ensure the whole group re-reads the sentence correctly.

4. If the puppet makes an error that is unnoticed, **say:** *Something didn't sound quite right to me. Let's re-read the page.* Keep the same error.

5. If the puppet makes an interesting mistake, point out how making a mistake changes the meaning of the sentence.

6. Finish by having the pupils read the whole story with the puppet listening to each pupil.

Key checks: Can the pupils track the text as it is read? Can the pupils spot errors and correct them?

Extension: Read a little more quickly and make a variety of mistakes, including decodable and unfamiliar words. The puppet could also say exception words as they are spelled, e.g. 'one' becomes 'own' or 'on-eh', 'people' becomes 'pee-op-le'.

Support: Limit mistaken words to words the pupil will find easy to spot to build confidence.

Prove it

Strand: Reading – comprehension

Learning objective: To be able to answer questions about the story and say what may happen next, including giving reasons.

You will need: a set of books that are the same (e.g. guided group reading books)

Note: It is important you have read the whole text before beginning the session. There is often a teacher's book to accompany guided group books. This is a useful source of questions.

1. **Say:** *Let's think about the book we are reading. We're going to think about the story and give reasons for what we think. Sometimes the ideas in a book may be a bit hidden, but I know you are fantastic reading detectives, and we will find them!*

2. Read the book together. Then ask the following questions, inviting responses and noting feedback.

3. **Ask:** *Can you find words to show how the character is feeling at the beginning of the story?*

4. **Ask:** *Can you find words to show what the mood of the story is at the beginning? Are there any words that reflect the mood in the setting?*

5. **Ask:** *Think about what the character does here. What does this tell you about them?* For example, the character may do something that reveals an unexpected quality, e.g. kindness in someone you thought was wicked.

6. **Ask:** *What problems do you think the characters may face? What makes you think this?* For example, you may think the characters are going to have a difficult journey, because they have to climb a mountain.

7. **Ask:** *How do you think the story might end? What makes you think this?* Ask this question more than once during the story. **Ask:** *Have you changed your mind about how you think the story might end? Why?*

Key checks: Can pupils find evidence in the story to support their answers?

Extension: Ask the pupils to write their answers, rather than just providing verbal feedback.

Support: Ask the pupils the questions one at a time, and help them to find the page that gives the answer. Explain that the words they need to find are on the page. **Say:** *Be a detective and examine the page carefully for word clues.*

What do you think?

Strand: Reading – comprehension

Learning objective: To discuss books, sharing opinions with others.

You will need: a selection of books

Note: This session will need to be repeated throughout the year as pupils gain knowledge of books.

1. **Say:** *Everyone select a favourite book or poem. You are going to say what you particularly liked about the book. Anyone else who has read the book, I would also like to know what you think.*

2. Praise pupils who actively listen during discussion. **Say:** *I could see you were listening to _____, as you were looking at her and nodding. Do you have anything else you'd like to say about this book?*

3. Try to take no more than three responses about a particular title or you will not hear about all the books.

4. Encourage pupils to be honest about a book. (e.g. Actually, I didn't particularly enjoy that book, as when I was little I was startled by an owl, so I prefer books without owls, even if they are very cute!)

5. **Ask:** *Who else should read this book and why would you recommend it to them?*

Key checks: Do the pupils understand that an opinion is personal and that there is no correct answer? Pupils need to learn that disliking a book is acceptable, as long as they can justify and give a reason for it.

Extension: Encourage pupils to apply their discussion to poetry.

Support: Give pupils sentence starters, **say:** *I like this part of the book because... My favourite character was... because...*

Beat the clock!

Strand: Writing – transcription

Learning objective: To spell by segmenting words into sounds.

You will need: pencils, paper/writing books, a clock/stopwatch, a tray with 10–15 objects or pictures on it (e.g. flower, shell, bird, monkey, worm, jar, badge, chimney, apple, towel, plant, ball, ice, knee, bridge)

1. **Say:** *When we segment words to spell them we need to chop them into their sounds.*

2. **Say:** *Look at this tray and choose an object* (e.g. flower). Make a chopping motion with your hand and **say:** *f-l-ow-er.* Repeat *f-l-ow-er* and count the sounds on your fingers.

3. **Say:** *First I will write 'f', next 'l', then 'ow', but should I use 'ou' or 'ow'? I will choose 'ow' because that looks right in 'flower'. Finally, 'er' – I can choose 'ir' 'er' or 'ur'. I will choose 'er' because I think that looks right. F-l-ow-er. Flower.*

4. **Ask:** *Can you choose another object from the tray, then say and count the sounds?*

5. Name every object on the tray, so all the pupils know all the words (nouns) they need to write. **Say:** *Now, beat the clock! Write down as many objects as possible in three minutes.*

6. **Say:** *Let's check the words together, counting how many sounds in each word. Make any corrections you need to.*

Key checks: Can the pupils write letters in response to the sound? Are the pupils segmenting the words properly? (Some pupils cannot hear that 'f-l' are two separate sounds.)

Extension: Select objects that are multisyllabic (e.g. paintbrush, squirrel, crayon) or give pupils less time.

Support: Select objects that pupils will be able to segment and spell independently (e.g. pen, peg, bin, lid).

Word twins

Strand: Writing – transcription

Learning objective: To learn some common homophones and near-homophones.

You will need: a whiteboard, whiteboard pen, board rubber, writing books/paper, pencils

1. **Say:** *A homophone is a word that sounds the same as another word but has a different meaning. You listen on a telephone; this can help you to remember that homophones are words that sound the same but look different. They sound like word twins.*

2. **Say:** *sea and see. Tell me about sea/see.* The pupils should give you two meanings – the deep blue sea, and you see with your eyes. Draw a simple illustration for each of these on your whiteboard. **Say:** *These words sound the same so they are homophones, but they have different meanings.* **Ask:** *What are the different ways of spelling the 'ee' sound?* Pupils should decide which ea/ee to use and write it into their books. Check together.

3. Repeat with other homophones: here/hear, bare/bear, to/two/too, sun/son, be/bee.

Key checks: Do the pupils know the different ways of spelling the same sound?

Extension: Use other homophones, e.g. knight/night, there/they're/their, blue/blew. Look at near homophones, e.g. quite/quiet. Ask pupils to write a sentence that uses each word, e.g. The knight rode his horse into battle. Stars can be seen at night.

Support: If pupils are unsure of how to spell sounds, write the sounds needed on a small whiteboard for reference.

Say it and spell it

Strand: Writing – transcription

Learning objective: To learn to spell some common exception words.

You will need: whiteboard, whiteboard pen, board rubber, paper, pencils

Note: Learning common exception words should be built into a spelling programme. Look, say, cover, write, check is commonly used as a method for pupils to practise their spellings. However, some pupils will need extra support with some words. Identify the words using the pupils' writing books.

1. **Say:** *We are going to practise writing a word that you might have been finding tricky to spell. Let's look at the word 'beautiful'.*

2. Write the word 'beautiful', saying each letter name as you write the word. **Say:** *Knowing your sounds doesn't always help as this word has some lousy letters.* Say the letter names 'b-e-a-u' then the syllables '-ti-ful'. Beautiful. **Ask:** *Can you write the word in the same way saying the letter names and sounds?*

3. **Say:** *Turn the whiteboard over and write the word again.* Check using the whiteboard. If it is incorrect, repeat step 2, and try again.

4. Put the word into a sentence and say the sentence, e.g. The sky was beautiful. **Say:** *Now you say the sentence.* **Ask:** *Can you write the sentence?* Check together.

Key checks: Can the pupils say the pattern of sounds and words?

Extension: Pupils should be able to correctly spell and use words from the Year 2 common exception words list, as the well as the school's spelling scheme.

Support: Ensure pupils are writing words on the Year 1 list correctly.

One word instead of two

Strand: Writing – transcription

Learning objective: To correctly spell and use the contracted forms of words.

You will need: whiteboards, whiteboard pens, board rubbers, flashcards with the contracted and uncontracted forms of words on them

1. **Ask:** *Can you write 'did not' on your whiteboard?* **Say:** *Most people say 'didn't' rather than 'did not'. To write 'didn't' we need to push the two words 'did' and 'not' together. While pushing the words together though, the 'o' falls out and gets replaced with an apostrophe. This shows there is a letter missing.* Rub out the 'o' and replace it with an apostrophe.

2. **Ask:** *Can you shorten the words 'did not' into 'didn't'?*

3. **Ask:** *Where did the 'o' go? What is that* (point to apostrophe) *called?*

4. **Say:** *Write 'has not' on your whiteboard.* **Ask:** *Can you shorten these two words?*

5. Repeat step 4 with could not (couldn't), it is (it's), I will (I'll). **Ask:** *How many letters have fallen out of the words?* **Say:** *So an apostrophe shows a missing letter or letters.*

6. **Say:** *Let's practise using the words in sentences.* For example, 'I'll have an apple please.'

Key checks: Can pupils correctly shorten words using an apostrophe? Do pupils understand the purpose of the apostrophe?

Extension: Write 'cannot' and 'can't' on a whiteboard. **Say:** *This is one word that has been shortened.* **Ask:** *Can you say which letters are missing?* **Say:** *Usually two words are pushed together, but in this case, it is one word that has been shortened.*

Support: Write the contracted and uncontracted forms onto flashcards for pupils to match. They can compare the two forms and spot the difference between the two forms. Draw attention to the missing letters and apostrophe by writing these in a different colour.

It's mine!

Strand: Writing – transcription

Learning objective: To learn to write and use the possessive apostrophe.

You will need: whiteboards, whiteboard pens, board rubbers, a selection of items (e.g. coat, book bag)

1. **Say:** *We are going to learn how to write about your belongings.* **Ask:** *Can you collect one item that belongs to you?*

2. Name each pupil's item in turn, e.g. coat, book bag, ball, recorder, PE kit.

3. Tell the pupils who owns each item, e.g. This PE kit belongs to Maya. This is Maya's PE kit. This ball belongs to Sarah. This is Sarah's ball. This coat belongs to Aswan. This is Aswan's coat.

4. Write both sentences on the whiteboard. Point out the order of the words: the common and proper nouns are reversed when using the possessive apostrophe. **Say:** *This apostrophe does not mean there are letters missing – no words have been contracted. This apostrophe shows belonging.*

5. **Ask:** *Can you use an apostrophe to write about each other's belongings?*

6. **Say:** *Now read out your sentence.* The pupil who is mentioned should hold up their item and say 'It's mine!', e.g. Sarah reads 'This is Maya's PE kit.' Maya holds the PE kit and says 'It's mine!'

Key checks: Do pupils understand that apostrophes have different purposes and contraction and possession are different? Watch out for pupils adding apostrophes to plural words ending with 's'.

Extension: Ask the pupils to use both types of apostrophe in their sentence: an apostrophe to show a shortened word, and an apostrophe to show possession, e.g. It's Aswan's coat. Can pupils change their other sentences?

Support: Ensure pupils are repeating the phrases before attempting to write them. Write the object words on a whiteboard, leaving space for the pupil to add the name and apostrophe.

Fix it on the end 1

Strand: Writing – transcription

Learning objective: To add suffixes to regular words to correctly spell longer words.

You will need: cards prepared with root words and suffixes (ideally the suffixes should be written on different coloured card), a pretend screwdriver, whiteboards, whiteboard pens, board rubbers

Note: It is suggested that two sessions are used to teach this objective. Session 1: -ly, -less and -ful. Session 2: -ment and -ness.

1. **Ask:** *Do you know what a suffix is?* Allow time for pupils to respond. **Say:** *A suffix is a letter or group of letters added to the end of a word, which slightly changes the meaning of the word.*

2. **Say:** *Let's look at the word 'bad' and the suffix '-ly'. Bad is an adjective. When the suffix -ly is added* (make a fixing-it-on action using the screwdriver), *it becomes an adverb (a word to describe a verb). For example, He drives badly. You can't say He drives bad.*

3. Take more root words, e.g. loud, bright, clever, final, and ask the pupils to add the suffix -ly. **Say:** *Can you write the adverb on your whiteboard?* They should make loudly, brightly, cleverly, finally.

4. **Say:** *This is another suffix, -less.* Demonstrate 'fixing on' the suffix -less to the word pain. **Ask:** *Can you add -less to these words: hope, thank, colour?* Pupils should make hopeless, thankless, colourless.

5. **Say:** *Adding the suffix -less to a word changes the meaning of the word to 'without' something. Thankless means 'without thanks'. Colourless means 'without colour'.* **Ask:** *Can you explain what painless means?*

6. **Say:** *This is another suffix, -ful.* Demonstrate 'fixing on' the suffix -ful to the word cheer. **Ask:** *Can you add -ful to these words: use, dread, thank, colour?* Pupils should make dreadful, thankful, colourful, useful.

7. **Say:** *Adding the suffix -ful to a word changes the meaning of the word to 'lots of' or 'full of' something. Thankful means 'lots of thanks'. Colourful means 'full of colour'.* **Ask:** *Can you say what cheerful means?*

8. **Say:** *This is another suffix, -ment.* Demonstrate 'fixing on' the suffix -ment to the word entertain. **Ask:** *Can you add -ment to these words: amaze, enjoy, pay, move?* Pupils should make amazement, enjoyment, payment and movement.

Continues

9. **Say:** *Adding the suffix -ment to a word changes a verb (an action word) into a noun. For example, to pay someone is an action, a payment is the money they get.* **Ask:** *Can you use entertain and entertainment in sentences?*

10. **Say:** *This is another suffix, -ness.* Demonstrate 'fixing on' the suffix -ness to the word fresh. **Ask:** *Can you add -ness to these words: bold, kind, wet, plain, ill?* Pupils should make boldness, kindness, wetness, plainness and illness.

11. **Say:** *Adding the suffix -ness makes the word into a noun to show a way of being. Boldness means 'being bold or brave'. Kindness means 'being kind'.* **Ask:** *Can you explain what freshness means?*

12. Make links between root words that are the same, but where different suffixes can be added. Look at 'cheer' and screw on different suffixes to change the meaning (-ful, -less). Look at 'help' and screw on different suffixes to change the meaning (-ful, -less). Look at 'helpful' and screw on different suffixes to change the meaning (-ness, -ly).

Key checks: Do pupils understand that adding a suffix alters the meaning of the root word?

Extension: Ask pupils to write sentences using the word.

Support: Break the session into smaller chunks so that one suffix is taught at a time.

Fix it on the end 2

Strand: Writing – transcription

Learning objective: To add suffixes to irregular words to correctly spell longer words.

You will need: cards prepared with root words and suffixes (ideally the suffixes should be written on different coloured card), a pretend screwdriver, whiteboards, whiteboard pens, board rubbers

Note: It is suggested two sessions are used to teach this objective. Session 1 -ly, -less and -ful. Session 2 -ment and -ness.

1. Re-cap from previous session. **Ask:** *Can you remember what a suffix is?* Allow time for pupils to respond. **Ask:** *What are the suffixes we have already learned about?* As each suffix is mentioned, reveal the card with it written on.

2. **Say:** *We are going to look at the same suffixes, but sometimes we need to change the spelling of the root word. You need to be spelling detectives and spot what happens.*

3. **Say:** *Here is the suffix -ly. It changes an adjective to an adverb. Can you add -ly to the words happy, day, rude, wise, crazy?* Pupils should make happily, daily, rudely, wisely and crazily. **Ask:** *What happens to the words?* **Say:** *There are two things. Either the suffix is added directly to the end of the word or the 'y' is replaced by an 'i' then the suffix is added.* Use a whiteboard to demonstrate rubbing out the 'y' and changing it to an 'i' then use the screwdriver to add the suffix.

4. **Say:** *Here is another suffix -less.* **Ask:** *How does it change the meaning of the word?* **Say:** *It changes the meaning to 'without' something.* Use the words mercy, rest, care, penny to make merciless, restless, careless, and penniless. **Ask:** *Do these words follow the same spelling rule?* Use a whiteboard to demonstrate rubbing out the 'y' and changing it to an 'i' then use the screwdriver to add the suffix.

5. **Say:** *Here is another suffix -ful.* **Ask:** *How does it change the meaning of the word?* **Say:** *It changes the meaning to 'lots of' or 'full of' something.* Use the words beauty, pity, force, plenty to make beautiful, pitiful, forceful and plentiful. **Ask:** *Do these words follow the same spelling rule?* Use a whiteboard to demonstrate rubbing out the 'y' and changing it to an 'i' then use the screwdriver to add the suffix.

Continues

6. **Say:** *Here is another suffix -ment.* **Ask:** *How does it change the meaning of the word?* **Say:** *It changes the word into a noun that is a way of being.* Use the words merry, improve, settle, treat and argue to make merriment, improvement, settlement, treatment and argument. **Ask:** *Do these words follow the same spelling rule?* Use a whiteboard to demonstrate rubbing out the 'y' and changing it to an 'i' then use the screwdriver to add the suffix. Note that argue loses 'e' before adding -ment.

7. **Say:** *Here is another suffix -ness.* Use the words greedy, hungry, crazy and happy to make greediness, hungriness, craziness and happiness. **Ask:** *Do these words follow the same spelling rule?* Use a whiteboard to demonstrate rubbing out the 'y' and changing it to an 'i' then use the screwdriver to add the suffix.

Key checks: Can pupils remember how suffixes alter the meaning of words?

Extension: Use a dictionary with support to learn the meanings of new words. Use these words in sentences.

Support: Break the session into smaller chunks so that one suffix is taught at a time.

Super spelling

Strand: Writing – transcription

Learning objective: To use knowledge of spelling rules to support spelling.

You will need: whiteboards, whiteboard pens, board rubbers, a puppet/class toy, sound mat, the following sentences prepared on strips of paper:
1. It was lait at knight and the dark, empty streat was quiet.
2. Everybodee was sleaping soundly in there beds.
3. Eeven the tall, stoan clock tower was still and silent.
4. Wet clothes hung limpley in the air.
5. A bold mouse wonted food and hungryly scurried to the wud.
6. With won gulp, an owl mercylessly eight it! Delishus!

1. **Say:** *You are now spelling experts, and I would like you to check these sentences, written by _____ the class puppet, for spelling mistakes.*

2. **Say:** *I am pleased with _____ the puppet because she has tried hard to write tricky words by using her sounds, but some of these words we definitely know how to spell.*

3. **Ask:** *Can you find the spelling errors within the sentence?* Model rewriting the sentence onto the whiteboard correctly.

4. **Ask:** *Can you choose a sentence each and write it out correctly onto your whiteboard?*

5. Check the sentences together.
   1. It was <u>late</u> at <u>night</u> and the dark, empty <u>street</u> was quiet.
   2. <u>Everybody</u> was <u>sleeping</u> soundly in <u>their</u> beds.
   3. <u>Even</u> the tall, <u>stone</u> clock tower was still and silent.
   4. Wet clothes hung <u>limply</u> in the air.
   5. A bold mouse <u>wanted</u> food and <u>hungrily</u> scurried to the <u>wood</u>.
   6. With <u>one</u> gulp, an owl <u>mercilessly ate</u> it! <u>Delicious</u>!

Key checks: Can pupils remember the spelling rules, knowledge of sounds and common exception words?

Extension: Number the sentences so they tell a short story.

Support: Select shorter sentences to start with. Underline the words with spelling errors to support identification. Use sound mats if required.

This is a sentence

Strand: Writing – transcription

Learning objective: To write a simple sentence from memory. (This will support pupils with their writing, as they will learn to construct a sentence orally, write it and check it.)

You will need: a whiteboard, whiteboard pen, paper, pencils, a coloured whiteboard pen, a stimulus for writing (e.g. an object or picture)

1. Look at an object, e.g. a plant. Orally compose a sentence about the object, e.g. 'Here is a plant with long leaves.' Ensure the sentence is a maximum of eight words.

2. Repeat the sentence, putting up a finger for each word you say. **Ask:** *Can you repeat the sentence? How many words do I need to write?*

3. Remind pupils that they need to start their sentence with a capital letter and end with a full stop. On their whiteboards ('punctuation holding box'), pupils write 'CAPITALS' and full stop. If other punctuation needs to be used, add it to the whiteboard. The punctuation holding box is a useful tool; as pupils use each punctuation type, they rub it out. When they have finished, if they have used all the punctuation needed, the box will be empty.

4. **Ask:** *Can you write the sentence on your whiteboard? Remember to use the punctuation.* If pupils appear stuck, **say:** *Say the sentence again. Now can you remember the next word?*

5. **Say:** *I would like you to check your work now, using a coloured pen. Tick every letter or punctuation mark that is in the right place and write in any you may have forgotten.* Model writing the sentence on the whiteboard, applying the punctuation and ticking it off as you go. Model your thought processes about spelling, breaking down words as needed. Pupils check and correct their own work.

6. Repeat for a second sentence.

Key checks: Are all the pupils joining in? Pupils who do not say the sentence aloud will find writing it more difficult. Are pupils remembering to refer to the punctuation holding box?

Extension: Add more complicated punctuation and multi-syllabic words. Try to keep to 8–9 words per sentence.

Support: Use a shorter sentence with more basic punctuation and commonly misspelt words. Provide a 'sound holding box' containing the digraphs required.

Jolly joins 1

Strand: Handwriting

Learning objective: To develop a joined handwriting style.

You will need: lined paper, pencils, a chart of the letters joined and unjoined

Note: Refer to your school's handwriting scheme, as schools approach handwriting in different ways. It is important that your school has a consistent approach to handwriting, by introducing letters in a particular order. Often handwriting and phonics schemes are linked. Most schools have a 'patter' (what to say for each letter), which helps young pupils develop good habits for forming letters.

1. Troubleshoot letters that pupils are having difficulty forming. **Say:** *I have noticed your letter ___ needs to be formed properly, because this will make it easier for you to join your letters.* Practise individual letters with pupils until they are secure. Build up to using the letter in a word, and finally, a sentence.

2. **Say:** *Now you are writing more sentences, it will be quicker if you can join your letters. It is important to be careful that your writing is still clear to read.*

3. When joining, encourage the pupils to keep letters sitting on the line. **Say:** *The first letter will decide the size of all the other letters on the line, so think before you start. A capital letter should be twice the height of a lower case letter, for example 'c'.*

4. **Say:** *Remember that capital letters are not joined. We also do not usually join the letter 'r' as it can easily be mistaken for 'n'.*

Key checks: Do pupils have an efficient grip on their pencil? Are they forming the letters correctly?

Extension: Ask pupils to write a sentence requiring all the letters of the alphabet. (This type of sentence is called a pangram.) For example, Jackdaws love my big sphinx of quartz. Crazy Frederick bought very many exquisite opal jewels. To support pupils with spelling, these could be written on a whiteboard unjoined.

Support: Pupils may require special handwriting paper, which has extra lines, to support them to size their letters. Pupils with a weak grip may also benefit from a pencil grip.

Jolly joins 2

Strand: Handwriting

Learning objective: To develop a joined handwriting style with letters of the correct size and orientation.

You will need: lined paper, pencils, a chart of the letters joined and unjoined, a completed piece of writing to publish, a watch with a second hand/a stopwatch

1. **Say:** *We are going to publish your story to go on our star writing display. Make sure your capital letters are twice the height of lower case letters, that you join as many letters as you can, and that you leave spaces between your words.*

2. Model the process by publishing a sentence and talking aloud about the handwriting process. **Say:** *I can see this is the start of the sentence, it starts with a capital letter, which I will not be joining. At the end of the word, I only need to leave a small gap, about the same size as a letter 'c', I don't need a gigantic gap. Now at the end of the sentence, I need to include the punctuation.* Include any talking about special punctuation, e.g. inverted commas, or spelling focus words.

3. As the pupils are working, give them specific praise for working on their handwriting, e.g. You have left just the right size space between these words. You have put the curly tail of that letter below the line just the right amount. I can see you are trying hard to join your letters today.

Key checks: Do pupils have an efficient grip on their pencil? Are they forming letters correctly?

Extension: Say: *Joined handwriting should make it easier for you to write both quickly and neatly. Let's have a handwriting race to see who can write a sentence in less than 30 seconds in their neatest joined handwriting.* Read out a pangram sentence (see previous activity). Time pupils for 30 seconds and evaluate their handwriting. Repeat the sentence, decreasing the amount of time, but still expecting the same quality.

Support: Pupils may require special handwriting paper, which has extra lines, to support them to size their letters. Pupils with a weak grip may also benefit from a pencil grip.

Listmania

Strand: Writing – vocabulary, grammar and punctuation

Learning objective: To use commas to separate items in a list.

You will need: a rucksack for packing, whiteboards, whiteboard pens, board rubbers, pencil, paper, smaller pieces of paper

1. **Say:** *We are going to pack a rucksack for an upcoming school trip.*
   Ask: *What should go in it? Draw and label these items on pieces of paper.*

2. **Say:** *A packing list is much easier to have than a whiteboard or lots of pieces of paper with drawings on. I can rewrite my list onto one piece of paper using commas to separate the items. A comma is a punctuation mark that indicates a short pause.*

3. **Say:** *As I write my items into a list, I need to separate each item with a comma, like this. Between the final two items, instead of a comma I'm going to use the word 'and'.*

4. Write an example on the whiteboard, e.g. First aid kit, water bottle, packed lunch, coat, class list, paper, pencil, camera, hat and gloves.

5. **Ask:** *What sort of letter does the first word of the sentence need to be?* (A capital letter.)

6. Practise writing lists, using commas to separate items, e.g. collections of objects or pupils' names in the group.

Key checks: Can the pupils correctly position a comma? Can the pupils use capital letters correctly? Do pupils remember to use 'and' between the final two items on the list?

Extension: A list has a purpose. Make this really clear by adding a title.
Ask: *When do you use a list? When have you seen lists being used?* Can pupils rewrite their list in alphabetical order?

Support: Tick items off the whiteboard as they are written down into a list using commas to separate each item. **Say:** *Let's write 'coat' first.* Tick 'coat' off on the whiteboard. **Say:** *Now, place your comma.* Next write 'hat'. Tick 'hat' off the whiteboard. Continue until all items have been written, remembering to use 'and' between the final two items.

Sentence types 1

Strand: Writing – vocabulary, grammar and punctuation

Learning objective: To learn how to use statement and question sentence types.

You will need: whiteboards, whiteboard pens, board rubbers, paper, pencil, a box containing a classroom object (e.g. a paintbrush)

1. **Ask:** *What is a sentence?* Give pupils time to respond. **Say:** *It is a group of words that are connected to each other. A sentence is usually marked with a capital letter at the beginning and a full stop at the end. It must contain a verb, otherwise it is just a phrase.*

2. **Say:** *A statement is a type of sentence that provides information. It also starts with a capital letter and ends with a full stop.* **Ask:** *Can you make a statement about your clothes?* (e.g. I am wearing black socks, trousers and a yellow shirt.) Pupils say a statement about their clothes.

3. **Ask:** *Can you write your statement? Remember to start with a capital letter and end with a full stop.* **Say:** *Let's swap statements. First, read it to yourself, then read it aloud to everyone.*

4. **Ask:** *Can you say what was good about the statement you read?* For example, they remembered to start with a capital letter and end with a full stop.

5. **Say:** *A question is asked to find out information. It is a type of sentence. It usually starts with a question word and ends with a question mark.*

6. **Ask:** *What are the question words?* Write the words on the whiteboard: what / where / who / when / why / how.

7. **Say:** *We are going to play a game. I have hidden an object in this box. You are going to take turns to ask questions to find out what is in the box.*

Key checks: Can pupils explain what a sentence is? Do pupils know that sentences begin with capital letters and end with punctuation, usually a full stop?

Extension: Ask pupils to write a statement about what another pupil in the room is wearing. Can the pupils in the group work out who the statement is describing?

Support: Have a 'punctuation holding box' containing the word CAPITALS and a full stop and question mark. Model writing your statement and erasing these. This will remind pupils to add their punctuation. Have question starters available, e.g. Do you use it for...? Can I get it myself? Where is it...?

Sentence types 2

Strand: Writing – vocabulary, grammar and punctuation

Learning objective: To learn how to use exclamation and command sentence types.

You will need: whiteboards, whiteboard pens, board rubbers, paper, pencil, a programmable robot, a helmet

Prepare the following sentences onto strips of paper for sorting.

Exclamation sentences	Sentences with exclamation marks
What an amazing day!	I can't believe you're seven already!
How thoughtless of him!	Stop being so noisy!
How sad the flowers didn't grow!	Hurry up, we are late!
What a huge cake!	Congratulations, you got the job!

1. **Say:** *An exclamation is another type of sentence. Exclamation sentences start with 'what' or 'how' and finish with an exclamation mark. Not all sentences that finish with an exclamation mark are exclamation sentences.*

2. **Say:** *Here are some sentences. Sort these sentences into exclamation sentences and other sentences using exclamation marks.*

3. **Ask:** *Can you think of an exclamation sentence starting with 'what' or 'how'? It will also usually contain a verb. Can you say your sentence out loud? Everyone else is going to repeat it. Now write each sentence.*

4. **Say:** *A command is another type of sentence. Commands are bossy and tell you what to do. They usually finish with a full stop. Commands usually start with a verb (an action word).*

5. **Say:** *Stand behind your chair. Touch your toes.* **Ask:** *What are the verbs in the sentences I just said?* (stand and touch) *A command gives an instruction.*

6. Show pupils a programmable robot. **Say:** *If you tell the robot what to do he will do it.* **Ask:** *Can you think of some command sentences for the robot to follow? The command should start with a verb, instruct the robot about what to do, and end with a full stop.* Check sentences together.

Continues

7. Take turns to put on the helmet and pretend to be a programmable robot. Other pupils give a command sentence and the robot follows it.

Key checks: Do pupils understand that there are different sentence types? Do pupils know what different punctuation looks like and how to use it appropriately? Do pupils understand what a verb is?

Extension: Write command sentences for the programmable robot to follow, e.g. instructions for how to get from this chair to the book corner, and use the robot to carry these out. Make sure they start with a verb and a capital letter and end with a full stop.

Support: Help pupils to think of exclamation sentences by giving them the start of the sentence, e.g. How funny that... How strange that... How incredible that... How terrible that.... With commands, give pupils a word bank of instruction words, such as move, turn, right, left, one step, two steps, stop.

Find the object

Strand: Writing – vocabulary, grammar and punctuation

Learning objective: To understand and write expanded noun phrases.

You will need: whiteboards, whiteboard pens, board rubbers, paper, pencil, different exercise books, a collection of small related objects (e.g. toy cars, small army characters)

1. **Ask:** *Can you explain what a noun is?* **Say:** *A noun is a naming word.* Point to different objects and say what they are, e.g. *pencil, table, book. These are all nouns.*

2. **Ask:** *Can you explain what an adjective is?* Take pupils' responses. **Say:** *An adjective is a word that describes nouns or feelings, e.g. green, tiny and sharp are adjectives that could describe a pencil.*

3. **Say:** *There is more than one book on the table. So that you know which book I want you to point to, I will add adjectives to describe the book.* Point to the large yellow book. **Ask:** *How did you know which book to point to?* Allow pupils time to think and take feedback. **Say:** *I used adjectives to describe the book.*

4. Show pupils the collection of objects. Allow them to have a short time to look at and talk about the objects. **Ask:** *Can you think of as many adjectives as possible for each object and write these on your whiteboard?*

5. Line the objects up and number them. **Ask:** *Can you write an expanded noun phrase (a phrase with a noun and at least one adjective) for one of the objects? Everyone else will guess which number your object is.*

6. **Say:** *It's time to play the quiz. Read out your expanded noun phrase, and everyone else will write down the object number.* Check through together.

Key checks: Do pupils understand what a noun is? Do pupils understand what an adjective is? Do pupils understand what an expanded noun phrase is?

Extension: Make the objects very similar so pupils need to be more precise with their descriptions, e.g. a collection of dolls all with blonde hair.

Support: Write a selection of adjectives on separate cards. They should fit the group of objects. **Say:** *I would like you to choose one adjective, e.g. red. Which of the objects could it describe?* Select the red objects and move them closer. **Say:** *Now choose another adjective, for example, stripy. Now which of the objects could it describe? So, these objects are red and stripy. Now write the noun phrase, the red, stripy car.*

Simple tenses

Strand: Writing – vocabulary, grammar and punctuation

Learning objective: To understand and use the simple past and present tenses.

You will need: whiteboards, whiteboard pens, board rubbers, paper, pencil, pretend microphone, the following prepared questions about school life (leave spaces between questions for pupils to write answers):

Where is your school?

What is your school called?

What is the best thing about your school?

Which class are you in?

What is your favourite lesson?

What are the school dinners like?

1. **Say:** *The past and present tenses are used in English to talk about events. The past tense is used to talk about events that have 'passed' and the present tense is used to talk about events that are happening now.*

2. **Ask:** *What did you do this morning?* Allow pupils time to discuss and take feedback. **Say:** *You have used verbs in the past tense to talk about what happened.* Write some of the sentences pupils said and underline the verb. Try and write down regular verbs only, e.g. eat/ate is irregular. Draw attention to the -ed ending, e.g. I play<u>ed</u> with my brother. I tidi<u>ed</u> my toys. I brush<u>ed</u> my teeth. I help<u>ed</u> get breakfast ready. **Ask:** *Can you write another sentence using the past tense about what you did this morning?*

3. **Ask:** *What did you do for your last birthday? Would you also use the past tense to talk about what happened?* (Yes, because it is also an event in the past.) **Ask:** *Can you write a sentence about your last birthday?* e.g. I visited a trampoline park with my friends.

4. **Ask:** *What did you do when you were a baby? Would you still use the past tense to talk about what happened?* Yes, because it is still an event in the past. **Ask:** *Can you write a sentence about when you were a baby?* e.g. When I was a baby, I toddled around the house.

Continues

5. **Say:** *The verbs we have looked at so far are regular. In the past tense they are easily spotted because they finish with -ed. Some verbs do not have an -ed ending in the past tense.* Give examples – eat/ate, draw/drew, drink/drank, sleep/slept. Write these on a whiteboard.

6. **Say:** *Imagine you are being interviewed for school TV. You are going to answer questions about classroom life to share with a school in another country. You will use the present tense to talk about yourselves.*

7. Use the microphone and ask each pupil a different question in 'interview style'. Ask the pupils to complete their answers to the questions on the sheet provided. Pupils could take turns to use the microphone and interview each other. If appropriate, the interview could be videoed.

Key checks: Do pupils understand that you use different tenses to talk about what has happened, compared to what is happening now? Do pupils realise that verbs can be regular or irregular?

Extension: Ask pupils to write full sentences and give lots of information about the school for their interview.

Support: Pupils may have fewer questions to answer. Encourage pupils to write in full sentences. You could split the session into two sessions: regular verbs and irregular verbs.

It's happening

Strand: Writing – vocabulary, grammar and punctuation

Learning objective: To understand and use the progressive forms of past and present tenses.

You will need: whiteboards, whiteboard pens, board rubbers, paper, pencil, pretend microphone, video of pupils playing/access to an outdoor area

1. **Say:** *Sometimes we want to talk about actions in progress. For example, I was feeding my cat last night, and she walked backwards into her water bowl! 'Was feeding' tells you about something happening at that time in the past.*

2. **Say:** *On the radio, football commentators tell listeners what is happening as the match is being played because the people listening want to know who has the ball and where the players are on the pitch. They talk very quickly because the action is so fast. I am going to comment on the action happening in the early years outdoor area. Use a 'commentator voice'. e.g. In the corner, Abbie is setting off on her scooter. She is riding safely, looking around as she goes. More action over there by the fence. Sadie and Malik are making a den with the big bricks. Thank you for listening.*

3. **Say:** *If we are talking about something happening in the past, we usually use 'was/were' + a verb. If it is something happening right now, we usually use 'is' + verb.*

4. **Ask:** *Can you observe what is happening in the classroom and write down what two pupils are doing?* e.g. Sian is writing in her book. Sati is sitting in the book corner.

5. **Ask:** *Can you watch the video of our sports day and write three sentences about what was happening?* e.g. The pupils were sprinting down the field. The reception class pupils were cheering.

Key checks: Do pupils understand the difference between the past and present? Do pupils understand when to use was/were? Are pupils able to use the progressive forms of verbs?

Extension: Pupils to write more than three sentences and improve their writing by adding expanded noun phrases.

Support: Pupils to say their sentence and have a go at writing it. Say and check the sentence together.

Coordinating cats

Strand: Writing – vocabulary, grammar and punctuation

Learning objective: To understand and use coordinating joining words.

You will need: whiteboards, whiteboard pens, board rubbers, paper, pencil, the following prepared pairs of sentences:

> The cat was starving. Her food bowl was empty.

> It is spaghetti and meatballs for lunch. Apple crumble and custard is for pudding.

> There is a tiny green shoot peeping through the soil. The plant must be getting ready to grow.

> I wonder if Thomas will go on the slide. Will he go on the swings first?

1. **Say:** *Joining words are used to make sentences longer and add more detail. We can use a joining word to join sentences that are about the same idea.*

2. Write the coordinating joining words on a whiteboard. **Say:** *'And' adds more information, 'so' gives the final idea, 'but' gives an unexpected idea, 'or' gives a choice.*

3. **Say:** *Let's test the different joining words out loud with the pairs of sentences. The cat was starving <u>and</u> her food bowl was empty.* (makes sense) *The cat was starving <u>but</u> her food bowl was empty.* (makes sense) *The cat was starving <u>or</u> her food bowl was empty.* (does not make sense) *The cat was starving <u>so</u> her food bowl was empty.* (does not make sense).

4. **Ask:** *Can you write the sentences using a joining word that makes sense? What needs to happen with the punctuation?* (Remove the first full stop and change the capital letter of the second sentence to a lower case letter.) If a pupil selects 'or' or 'so', discuss with them the meaning of the sentence.

5. Repeat with other pairs of sentences.

Key checks: Are pupils secure with the concept of a sentence? This is important or they will not understand that the punctuation needs to be changed when they join the sentences. Do pupils understand the role of coordinating joining words (and, but, so, or)?

Extension: Ask pupils to say what type of sentences are used in the examples (statements). Can pupils identify any expanded noun phrases?

Support: Have the first sentence written in advance, so the pupil needs to add the joining word and second sentence.

Subordinating squirrels

Strand: Writing – vocabulary, grammar and punctuation

Learning objective: To understand and use subordinating joining words.

You will need: whiteboards, whiteboard pens, board rubbers, paper, pencil, the following prepared pairs of sentences and phrases:

> I went home from school early _____ I was unwell.
>
> It was amazing ____the polar bear suddenly leaped into the water.
>
> We are going to finish this project _____ the special clay is delivered.
>
> Let's go fishing _____ we can collect shells.

1. Explain to pupils that joining words are used to make sentences longer and add more detail. **Say:** *We can use a joining word to join a sentence and an extra group of words, which is called a subordinate group of words. A subordinate group of words will add more detail to the main sentence. For example, let's look at the sentence, I had to turn off the television because it was time for a bath. 'I had to turn off the television' is a sentence. 'Because it was time for a bath' is not a sentence, it is a subordinate group of words. A subordinate group of words starts with a subordinate joining word or conjunction.*

2. Write the subordinating joining words on the whiteboard: because, when, if, and that. **Say:** *A group of words that contains a subordinate joining word is called subordinate. The other words are the main sentence. The subordinate joining words all tell us different things. 'Because' explains why something happens, 'when' gives a time, 'if' gives unexpected information and 'that' provides results.*

3. **Say:** *Let's test the different joining words out loud with some sentences and phrases. For example, We are going to finish this project, <u>because</u> the special clay is delivered. We are going to finish this project, <u>if</u> the special clay is delivered. We are going to finish this project, <u>that</u> the special clay is delivered. We are going to finish this project, <u>when</u> the special clay is delivered. Do all of these answers make sense?*

4. Give pupils the prepared pairs of sentences and phrases and ask them which subordinating joining word they think will fit in the gaps.

Continues

5. **Ask:** *Can you write some more sentences using a joining word that makes sense? Try and think of some sentences with more than one option.*

Key checks: Do pupils understand the concept of a sentence? Do they understand that a subordinate group of words does not make sense on its own? Do pupils understand the role of subordinate joining words (because, when, if, that)?

Extension: Say: *The subordinate clause can be before or after the main. I can move the entire subordinate clause to the front, like this. When I was unwell, I went home from school.* **Ask:** *Can you write sentences using the subordinate joining word 'when' at the beginning, e.g. When it is sunny...' or 'When there is time...'* **Say:** *You will need to make sure you have your capital letter and full stop in the correct places. After the subordinate clause, you also need to put a comma.*

Support: Have the main sentence already prepared on paper so pupils need to write the subordinate group of words. Orally play with the sentence, swapping the main and subordinate parts around. It is easier if the main and subordinate are on different strips of paper.

Standard English

Strand: Writing – vocabulary, grammar and punctuation

Learning objective: To recognise and use features of Standard English.

You will need: whiteboard, whiteboard pens, board rubbers, paper, pencils, the following prepared sentences:

Standard English	Non-Standard English	Corrected sentences using Standard English
The car drove without its lights on.		
The pupils sat under the tree.		
The plant grew very quickly.		
	The boy wasn't going nowhere.	The boy is going nowhere. The boy wasn't going anywhere.
	The man wasn't doing nothing.	The man is doing nothing. The man wasn't doing anything.
	The dinner should of been hotter.	The dinner should have been hotter.

1. **Say:** *Standard English is a way of speaking and writing correctly using English.*

2. Show the pupils the sentences from the Standard English and non-Standard English columns above. **Ask:** *Can you read the sentences and sort them into Standard English and non-Standard English?*

3. **Say:** *These sentences are written using Standard English.* Place them to one side. **Say:** *These sentences do not sound quite right. They have been written using non-Standard English. Let's look at this one. 'The boy wasn't going nowhere.'* **Ask:** *Which part of the sentence sounds strange?* **Say:** *It would be Standard English to say either 'The boy is going nowhere' or 'The boy wasn't going anywhere.'*

4. **Ask:** *Can you rewrite the other non-Standard English sentences in Standard English?* Check the sentences together.

Key checks: Can pupils find the errors in the non-Standard English sentences? Can pupils correct the errors to change the sentences to Standard English?

Extension: Work independently to correct the sentences.

Support: Underline the part of the sentence that is non-standard to support pupils in identifying this.

Let's talk about it

Strand: Writing – vocabulary, grammar and punctuation

Learning objective: To discuss writing using the correct grammatical terminology for Year 2.

You will need: pieces of the pupils' writing to discuss, whiteboard, whiteboard pen, board rubber

1. **Say:** *Today we are going to talk about _____ using our writing.* Select one aspect of grammar to discuss per session. The session will need to be repeated a number of times to cover all the grammar.

2. **Say:** *We are going to discuss the tenses* (or chosen grammatical strand) *in our writing today.* Write the chosen grammatical word on the whiteboard to refer to.

3. **Ask:** *Who has used a fantastic expanded noun phrase? Who has used an exclamation sentence type? Who thinks they have correctly used an apostrophe? Why did you use it? For a contraction or possession?*

4. Pupils should respond with comments about their writing. e.g. I am particularly pleased with my expanded noun phrase in this sentence because I remembered a great word we used before, and it fitted here. Read the sentence aloud.

Key checks: Can pupils use grammatical terminology correctly and with confidence? Are pupils able to use examples from their written work to demonstrate understanding?

Extension: Ask pupils to find further examples in books.

Support: Remind pupils what the grammatical term means in words they understand, using a whiteboard if necessary. For example, an exclamation sentence type starts with 'what' or 'how', usually contains a verb and ends with an exclamation mark.

Lost!

Strand: Writing – composition

Learning objective: To develop a positive attitude and stamina for writing by writing about a personal experience.

You will need: a cuddly toy or puppet that is well liked, paper, pencils, whiteboard, whiteboard pen, board rubber; optional: stories about getting lost, for example *Dogger* by Shirley Hughes

1. **Say:** *We are going to write a story today. It is about our class puppet.* Begin to look around the room and realise out loud that it cannot be found. Pre-arrange with another adult to have this hidden prior to beginning the session. It can be in or out of the classroom.

2. **Say:** *I'm a bit worried about the puppet now. I really wanted to use it in our writing today and write some adventures. Where can it be?* Lead discussion from the pupils about where the toy could be. For example, who else visits our classroom and may have borrowed it? If appropriate, visit places where it could be, e.g. the main office, the staffroom, the hall, a neighbouring classroom. Discover the toy and take it back to the classroom.

3. **Say:** *Now we can write about the adventures our toy has had! I thought we had lost him for good! I'm so relieved!*

4. Prepare the whiteboard by drawing a simple eye, ear, nose, hand and heart. **Ask:** *What do you think our toy has seen? Heard? Smelled? Touched?* Write the pupils' ideas on a whiteboard next to the appropriate drawing. **Ask:** *How do you think he/she felt?* Write pupils' ideas next to the heart. **Say:** *Let's make up a reason why he/she was not in our classroom. Perhaps he went to look for...?* Write pupils' ideas.

5. Model writing sentences from the pupils' ideas. For example:

   Arthur went to look for a piece of cheese, but got lost. He started to look around him and could see the brightly coloured walls of a classroom, but it wasn't the right room. He heard the chatter of pupils' voices, but they weren't the right voices. He smelled the fruit in the bowl, but it wasn't the right bowl. Arthur felt hopeless and miserably sat under a box. He desperately wanted to be found. Finally, his ears pricked up and he heard his class searching. They found him, cuddled him and brought him back.

Continues

95

6. **Ask:** *Have you ever been lost? Where were you? What happened?* Ask pupils to think about what they could see, hear, smell and touch. Ask pupils to make notes next to simple symbols on their paper. **Say:** *Where were you? Who found you? How did you feel?*

7. **Say:** *Now it's your turn to write about being lost using your notes.* You may wish to do this in a second session.

Key checks: Can pupils join in with the discussion? Pupils who are not active participants will find writing about their experience more difficult.

Extension: Provide types of words the pupils need to include in their writing, e.g. adjectives or adverbs. Provide a word mat with common exception words they can use to ensure they spell words correctly.

Support: Compose sentences together and ask the pupil to repeat the sentence until they have memorised it. Sit near the pupil and encourage them to be independent by saying 'What's next?' Where the pupil is unsure, re-read the words they have written to jog their memory.

An amazing thing happened...

Strand: Writing – composition

Learning objective: To write about a real-life event.

You will need: photographs, pencil, paper, a whiteboard, whiteboard pen, board rubber, a spinner (optional)

1. If possible, attend the event you would like the pupils to write about. This could be a visitor coming to school, visiting a wildlife area or space within the school grounds, a class trip, a charity event within the school or a sports day.

2. Show the pupils photographs of the event you would like them to write about, e.g. a charity event. **Ask:** *What happened on this day? Why did pupils come to school wearing pyjamas? What else happened within school? Which charity did we raise money for? What will the charity do with the money?* Write pupils' ideas on the whiteboard. It is important for all pupils to share their ideas. You could have a spinner on the table to point to who will contribute an idea, or pupils' names on lollysticks to ensure all pupils are participating.

3. Organise the ideas into chronological order, to ensure no parts of the event are left out. **Say:** *Remember to say your sentence out loud before you write it* down. Repeat each sentence before adding a further sentence. Point to each numbered section of the whiteboard to further support pupils.

4. **Ask:** *What was your favourite moment?* Look at the photographs and ask each pupil in the group what their favourite part of the day was. Ensure they phrase this as a sentence. Add this sentence to the piece of writing.

5. For example, *My favourite moment in the day was the candlelit assembly as I have never seen so many candles. It was very memorable.*

Key checks: Can pupils talk about their favourite event? Are pupils using their knowledge of sounds and common exception words to support spelling?

Extension: Encourage pupils to describe one activity within the event. Encourage pupils to structure their work into paragraphs and use subheadings.

Support: Pupils may need sentence starters to help them write, for example, 'Pupils at Riverside Primary School held a day of...'

Sense the seasons

Strand: Writing – composition

Learning objective: To write simple seasonal poems.

You will need: paper prepared with symbols for each of the senses, pencils

1. **Say:** *Poetry can take many forms. At its simplest, it can be thought of as word play. You can play around with the order of the words in poems, which you cannot do if you are writing a story.*

2. **Say:** *Let's go outside to closely observe the season.* **Ask:** *Can you use your senses to explore? Can you think of some descriptive words and phrases? What can you see? What can you hear? What can you smell? What can you feel? What can you taste?* **Say:** *You must not pick berries to eat, unless you have asked an adult. Berries are for birds.*

3. Return to the classroom. On prepared paper with symbols to represent the senses, write some descriptive words and phrases together, e.g. crunchy brown leaves, fir cones in perfect patterns, brightly coloured berries.

4. Share the following poem frame with the pupils:

   I love the sight of…
   I love the smell of…
   I love the sound of…
   I love the feel of…
   I love the taste of…

5. **Say:** *Now it's your turn to write a senses poem.* Pupils can arrange the order of the sentences as they wish.

Key checks: Are pupils using all their senses to think about and describe the season?

Extension: Ask pupils to imagine they are an animal living in that season, e.g. a rabbit in spring, a butterfly in summer, a squirrel in autumn, an owl in winter. **Say:** *Let's think again about using our senses while imagining we are this animal.* Add words and phrases to their paper.

Support: Simplify the poem frame.

I see…
I smell…
I hear…
I touch…
I taste…

Let's write

Strand: Writing – composition

Learning objective: To understand that writing is used for different purposes.

You will need: an early reader picture book, a shopping list, a leaflet, a letter, a newspaper, a picture book, a paperback book, an encyclopedia

1. Show pupils the collection of resources. **Say:** *Writing is used for many purposes. For example, it can help people to remember. Which type of writing that you can see here helps someone remember? Yes, the shopping list. Which type of writing gives information? Yes, the letter, newspaper or encyclopedia.*

2. **Say:** *Let's write a letter to a friend in another class. You are going to tell your friend something you have enjoyed learning about.* **Ask:** *How will you make sure your friend will be able to understand your writing?*

3. **Say:** *Let's write a picture book for a very young pupil that teaches the pupil about opposites.* **Ask:** *What do we need to include in this book?* Bold images and only one or two words on a page. *Who will need to be able to read your writing?* The parent or family member as very young pupils cannot read.

4. **Say:** *Let's write a shopping list of ingredients.* **Ask:** *How will you write what we need? Who needs to be able to read your writing?* An adult may need to read your writing if you are helping them by writing the shopping list.

5. **Say:** *Let's write a page for our class welcome book.* **Ask:** *What do visitors to our class need to know? Who will need to read your writing?*

6. Discuss all the different types of writing you have looked at. **Say:** *The person who will read your writing is called the audience.*

Key checks: Are pupils aware of the audience they are writing for? Vocabulary and size of handwriting will need to be taken into consideration. You may wish to split the session into two or more sessions and provide a checklist of features for the type of writing.

Extension: Pupils write a letter to their headteacher saying what they like about school and what they would like to change.

Support: Provide a writing frame or sentence starters to support pupils. If pupils are able to write independently, but do not have stamina to write a lot, write a question to them which they need to reply in writing to. For example, **say:** *Tell me more about the learning experience you enjoyed. What made that learning experience your favourite?* Expect properly punctuated sentences.

What a character!

Strand: Writing – composition

Learning objective: To create a plan to support writing.

You will need: a person shape on a piece of paper, pencils, a storybook with an interesting character, a whiteboard, whiteboard pen, board rubber

1. **Say:** *Our writing activity today is to describe a character on the outside and the inside. The outside of the character will be what the character looks like. The inside of the character is how they behave; if they are a kind or wicked character.*

2. Read the story and discuss the main character.

3. **Say:** *Around the outside of the person shape, you are going to write phrases to describe what the character looks like.* Use the illustrations to support the pupils to describe and write expanded noun phrases about the character. For example, *old brown sandals.* Introduce new vocabulary to the pupils. **Say:** *The sandals were not just old, they were 'ancient'.* Write ancient on a whiteboard.

4. **Say:** *Inside the person shape, you are going to write phrases to describe what the character is like.* Introduce new vocabulary to the pupils. **Say:** *The character wasn't just kind, he was gracious.* Write 'gracious' on a whiteboard.

5. Use the plan to support writing sentences about the character. Read through the writing together and check pupils have included capital letters and full stops to mark their sentences.

6. This piece of writing could be used for the 'Make it even better' activity later in the book. Ensure pupils leave an extra line between each line of writing to allow sufficient space for editing. **Say:** *Remember to write a line, miss a line.*

Key checks: Can pupils think of expanded noun phrases to describe what a character looks like? Can pupils think of words and phrases to describe what the character is like?

Extension: Choose a contrasting character from the book. This may be a 'baddie' character or a secondary character. Pupils will need to use inferential information to complete the person shape as before.

Support: Say and write sentences together, before pupils write sentences in their books. Provide sentence starters, e.g. At the beginning of the story, the character wore…

Change the story

Strand: Writing – composition

Learning objective: To create a plan to support writing.

You will need: a story mountain (you can draw this very simply on paper), pencils, a traditional story

1. **Say:** *Our writing activity today is to create a plan for a story based on a traditional tale. We will use the story mountain to help us plan our story.*

2. Read the story. **Say:** *Many words and phrases are repeated in this story. If you know the repeated phrase, please join in.*

3. **Ask:** *Let's think about what happens at each part of the story. What happens at the beginning? Middle? End?*

4. Add notes to the story mountain at appropriate points.

   Beginning: Main character introduced. Setting described. Problem outlined.
   On the way up: The problem becomes worse.
   Middle: Something happens to expose the problem.
   On the way down: Ideas to solve problem.
   End: The problem is solved, the characters end up happy.

5. **Say:** *We understand this story, so now we are going to change it a little. Let's change the problem.* Allow time for pupils to discuss and take feedback.

6. **Say:** *You are going to make notes on your own story plan to use when you rewrite the story.*

7. **Say:** *Remember each step of the mountain. You are only changing the problem, everything else – character and setting, will remain the same.*

8. **Ask:** *How will the characters solve this new problem?* Allow time for pupils to discuss and take feedback. **Say:** *Now complete your story mountain.*

Key checks: Can pupils organise their words and phrases to support writing?

Extension: Ask pupils to add speech for their characters.

Support: All pupils write about the same idea in Step 6. They then will write the same story, which can be supported in a guided way if required.

Write my own story

Strand: Writing – composition

Learning objective: To use the story mountain to write their own version of the traditional tale.

You will need: the story mountain created in the previous lesson, pencils, writing paper

1. **Say:** *We are going to write our own version of the story using our story mountains.*

2. Model how to use the story mountain to support writing. **Say:** *I need to start at the bottom of the story mountain, with introducing the main character. That will be my first sentence.* Write this sentence. Model re-reading the sentence. **Say:** *This is the very beginning of the story. How do traditional tales begin? I need to add in 'Once…' or 'Once upon a time…'* Insert this phrase at the appropriate place.

3. Continue modelling the beginning of the story in this way, including describing the setting and outlining the problem. **Ask:** *Can you write the beginning of your story?*

4. Think about the middle part of the story and ask questions to draw out what happens at this point. The details should be on the story mountain plan to support writing. **Say:** *Write the middle part of the story.*

5. Think about the end of the story and ask questions to check pupils' understanding. **Say:** *Write the end of the story.*

6. This piece of writing could be used for the next 'edit and improve' activity. Ensure pupils leave an extra line between each line of writing, to allow sufficient space for editing. **Say:** *Remember to write a line, miss a line.*

Key checks: Can pupils use their story mountain plan to support independent writing?

Extension: Allow pupils to continue writing at their own pace. Ask them to include expanded noun phrases and adverbs and to write some dialogue.

Support: Model the middle and end of the story if required. Support pupils with sentence starters to help them structure their story.

Make it even better

Strand: Writing – composition

Learning objective: To edit and improve a piece of writing.

You will need: a sample piece of writing or the character description from the 'What a character!' activity, a pen/pencil in a different colour, in line with the school's marking and feedback policy

1. **Say:** *You are going to check your writing to make sure you have punctuated all your sentences correctly. Check your sentences all start with a capital letter and end with a full stop or other appropriate punctuation.* Pupils should use a different colour to add in any punctuation that has been missed.

2. **Say:** *You are going to improve the writing by adding some more adverbs. We need to write how this character moves. We can add an adverb to show how this character is feeling when they are walking. He could walk happily, or quickly.* **Ask:** *Can you add an adverb to show how a character is feeling as they move?*

3. **Say:** *You are going to improve the writing by adding some more adjectives. We need to know exactly what this object looks like, because it is important in the writing. Can you add adjectives and change the writing into an expanded noun phrase? Can you use commas to list two adjectives?*

4. Listen to pupils' ideas and select one to add into the modelled piece of writing. **Say:** *Luckily, I left a line, so it is easy to add in this extra sentence.*

Key checks: Can pupils read their own writing? If pupils use too many ideas from the modelled piece, they do not have ownership of the writing, and are often not able to read it.

Extension: Ask pupils to add extra adjectives to describe. You could support pupils to use a thesaurus to look up synonyms to make their writing more interesting.

Support: Support pupils with reading their writing to a partner. Use your voice to support pupils to check for full stops by pausing where full stops should be.

Read it

Strand: Writing – composition

Learning objective: To read own writing to check it makes sense.

You will need: a piece of writing written by the pupil, a pen/pencil in a different colour, in line with the school's marking and feedback policy

1. **Say:** *You are going to check your writing makes sense by reading it out loud to the person next to you.* One pupil should place their writing face down and listen to the other pupil read their writing. They should then swap roles.

2. **Say:** *If you realise you have missed a word or something doesn't sound quite right, you can edit that part with your coloured pen.* The pupil who is listening may also offer support by suggesting extra words to add or ways of changing the word order as necessary.

3. Once all the editing and proofreading has been completed, **ask:** *Can you read your best sentence to the group?*

Key checks: Can pupils read their own writing? Are partners being supportive?

Extension: Pupils to read each other's writing out loud. This will allow the author to hear their own writing.

Support: Have the pupil read a sentence and then take it in turns repeating it until it is read fluently. Practise reading with expression so the pupil is able to read their own work with confidence.